Liquidity Management

For other titles in the Wiley Finance series please see
www.wiley.com/finance

Liquidity Management

A Funding Risk Handbook

ALDO SOPRANO

WILEY

This edition first published 2015
© 2015 Aldo Soprano

Registered office
John Wiley & Sons Ltd, The Atrium, Southern Gate, Chichester, West Sussex, PO19 8SQ, United Kingdom

For details of our global editorial offices, for customer services and for information about how to apply for permission to reuse the copyright material in this book please visit our website at www.wiley.com.

The right of the author to be identified as the author of this work has been asserted in accordance with the Copyright, Designs and Patents Act 1988.

Wiley publishes in a variety of print and electronic formats and by print-on-demand. Some material included with standard print versions of this book may not be included in e-books or in print-on-demand. If this book refers to media such as a CD or DVD that is not included in the version you purchased, you may download this material at http://booksupport.wiley.com. For more information about Wiley products, visit www.wiley.com.

Designations used by companies to distinguish their products are often claimed as trademarks. All brand names and product names used in this book are trade names, service marks, trademarks or registered trademarks of their respective owners. The publisher is not associated with any product or vendor mentioned in this book.

Limit of Liability/Disclaimer of Warranty: While the publisher and author have used their best efforts in preparing this book, they make no representations or warranties with respect to the accuracy or completeness of the contents of this book and specifically disclaim any implied warranties of merchantability or fitness for a particular purpose. It is sold on the understanding that the publisher is not engaged in rendering professional services and neither the publisher nor the author shall be liable for damages arising herefrom. If professional advice or other expert assistance is required, the services of a competent professional should be sought.

Library of Congress Cataloging-in-Publication Data
Soprano, Aldo.
  Liquidity management : a funding risk handbook / Aldo Soprano.
      pages cm. – (The wiley finance series)
    Includes bibliographical references and index.
    ISBN 978-1-118-41399-9 (hardback) – ISBN 978-1-118-41396-8 (ebk) –
ISBN 978-1-118-41398-2 (ebk)   1. Bank liquidity.   2. Risk management.   I. Title.
  HG1656.A3S66 2015
  658.15′5–dc23

                                                                    2015002039

A catalogue record for this book is available from the British Library.

ISBN 978-1-118-41399-9 (hbk)   ISBN 978-1-118-41396-8 (ebk)

ISBN 978-1-118-41398-2 (ebk)   ISBN 978-1-119-08794-6 (ebk)

Cover Design: Wiley
Cover Image: ©Getty Images/Steve Rawlings

Set in 11/13pt Times by Aptara Inc., New Delhi, India
Printed in Great Britain by TJ International Ltd, Padstow, Cornwall, UK

Contents

Acknowledgements   xi

Introductory Note   xiii

CHAPTER 1
Funding and Market Liquidity   1

1.1   Liquidity in the Financial Markets   1
    1.1.1   Definition of funding and liquidity risks   4
1.2   Managing Liquidity Risk   9
    1.2.1   Liquidity risk's framework   9
    1.2.2   Chief Risk Officer's role   15
1.3   Regulatory Frameworks   15
    1.3.1   Total net cash outflows   21
    1.3.2   Long-term funding requirements   22
    1.3.3   Banks' funding   23
    1.3.4   Funding through securitization   26
    1.3.5   Behavioural changes of customers or
          investors   28
    1.3.6   Payment systems   29
    1.3.7   Correspondent and custody activities   30
    1.3.8   Accounting treatment and liquidity   31
    1.3.9   Diversification of funding sources   31
    1.3.10   Rating agency approaches to internal
           methodologies   32

1.3.11 Transparency to the market   32
1.3.12 Contingency plans   33

CHAPTER 2
Short-Term Funding   **37**

2.1   Cash Flow Ladder   37
      2.1.1   Contractual cash flows   40
      2.1.2   Rules for mapping flows on the maturity
              ladder   42
      2.1.3   Flows without contractual certainty   42
      2.1.4   Unexpected cash flows   43
      2.1.5   Funds available for refinancing   44
      2.1.6   Funds transferability   44
      2.1.7   Total ladder calculation   44
2.2   Liquidity Coverage Ratio   45
      2.2.1   Regulatory prescriptions   45
      2.2.2   Liquid assets available for refinancing 46
      2.2.3   Total net cash outflows in the upcoming
              month   51
2.3   Liquidity Risk Indicators   58
      2.3.1   Using indicators   59
      2.3.2   Testing indicators   60
      2.3.3   Government bond yield curves and
              cross-spreads   61
      2.3.4   Credit default swap levels   61
      2.3.5   Foreign exchange cross-values   61
      2.3.6   Central bank refinancing   62
      2.3.7   Crisis indicators   62
      2.3.8   Risk aversion indexes   65
2.4   Intraday Liquidity Risk   66
      2.4.1   Intraday liquidity management   67
      2.4.2   Cooperative mechanism   71

		Analysing the possible impact of the stressed	
	2.4.3	scenario on intraday liquidity risk	73
	2.4.4	Haircuts to pledges	75
	2.4.5	Monitoring requirements	76
	2.4.6	Structural and intraday liquidity needs	76
	2.4.7	Payment systems' liquidity saving features	78
	2.4.8	Intraday liquidity risk in the case of Lehman	
		Brothers	79
	2.4.9	Some intraday liquidity monitoring indicators	80
	2.4.10	Intraday liquidity stress scenarios	82
2.5	Funding Concentration		83
	2.5.1	Significant counterparties	85
	2.5.2	Significant instruments/products	86
	2.5.3	Significant currencies	86
	2.5.4	Time buckets	87
2.6	Measuring Asset Liquidity		87
	2.6.1	Standard liquidity ratio	89
	2.6.2	Determining implied spread	90

CHAPTER 3
Long-Term Balance

			93
3.1	Structural Funding		94
	3.1.1	Determining the available funding	95
	3.1.2	Required stable funding for assets	97
3.2	Customer Deposit Modelling		99
	3.2.1	Regulatory approaches on deposit stability	103
	3.2.2	Depositor behaviours	104
	3.2.3	Modelling assumptions and impacts on	
		funding costs	106
	3.2.4	Dynamic regression models	109
3.3	Stress Testing and Scenario Analysis		111
	3.3.1	Using stress testing to improve banks' own	
		risk governance	112

3.3.2   Liquidity stress testing rationale   113
3.3.3   Improving controls   117
3.3.4   Stress testing methodology   117
3.3.5   Reverse stress testing   118
3.3.6   Scenario analysis   119
3.3.7   Internal capital and stress testing   122

CHAPTER 4
Liquidity Value At Risk   **123**

4.1   Market Liquidity Effects   123
        4.1.1   Market volatility   124
4.2   Market Liquidity Value At Risk   124
4.3   VaR Liquidation-Adjusted   133
        4.3.1   Exogenous and endogenous liquidity risk in
                   the VaR model   137
        4.3.2   Liquidity risk horizons   138
4.4   Cash Flows At Risk   140

CHAPTER 5
Control Framework   **143**

5.1   Governance Principles   143
5.2   Control Processes   148
        5.2.1   Functions in charge of liquidity risk
                   management and control   150
        5.2.2   Risk committees   151
        5.2.3   Coordinating liquidity management   152
        5.2.4   Liquidity risk monitoring function   153
        5.2.5   Addressing documentation-related liquidity
                   risks   154
5.3   Monitoring Liquidity Exposure   155
        5.3.1   Available assets for refinancing   156
        5.3.2   Funding concentration   157

| | | 5.3.3 | Liquidity coverage ratio and NSFR in the various currencies | 157 |

5.3.3 Liquidity coverage ratio and NSFR in the
various currencies 157
5.3.4 Market-related monitoring tools 158
5.3.5 Overall market information 158
5.3.6 Information on the financial sector 159
5.3.7 Company-specific information 160
5.3.8 Recommendations on the monitoring process 160
5.3.9 Reporting frequency and distribution 160
5.4 Setting Liquidity Risk Limits 161
5.4.1 Limit setting and review 162
5.4.2 Reporting and escalation procedures 163
5.4.3 Internal rules on limit setting and
management 164
5.5 Contingency Liquidity Plan 164
5.5.1 Outlining the contingency funding plans 167
5.5.2 Internal procedures for CFP 168

CHAPTER 6
Conclusions **169**

6.1 Funding Liquidity 169
6.2 Profitability Impact of Larger Counterbalancing
Asset Stocks 170
6.3 Pricing and Liquidity 171
6.4 Lessons Learnt 171

Bibliography **173**

Index **181**

Acknowledgements

In hoping this text is of interest and help in assessing and understanding liquidity risk, my first and greatest debt of gratitude goes to Werner Coetzee, Executive Commissioning Editor at Wiley, for suggesting and inspiring me to write it, but mostly for holding me to completing it when my first son's arrival kindly changed my private life and free time. A special mention is also owed to Carlo Magnani for his previous support and contribution. Lastly, I want to mention the many people over these difficult past years that have worked together with me on liquidity risk and deserve to be mentioned, without order or priority: Gianni Capezzuoli, Mario Prodi, Elena Conserva and Attilio Napoli.

The opinions and indications presented in this book are those of its author and do not represent that of UniCredit Group.

This book is dedicated to my wife Tanya and my son Andrea. And to the Lighthouse for showing us the way.

Introductory Note

This book was first conceived of and begun two years ago, at the peak of what it is now commonly referred to as the Greek financial crisis. As many well remember, it was the nadir of the financial crisis, triggered by the chain of problems from Ireland, Portugal and then Greece, resulting in state rating downgrades and endless discussions in Brussels and Frankfurt about the way to solve the apparently unresolvable liquidity troubles. All this while the Lehman crisis was barely one year old. Then the contagion fear that affected the Republic of Italy, one the largest sovereign debt issuers in the world, spread and the troubles quickly also reached Spain, with the Bankia and Spanish banking sectors in dire straits and receiving European financial help. Many governments fell, dragged down by extremely high refinancing costs, unemployment rates and falling growth rates.

Things have changed since. Mario Draghi's appointment at the helm of the European Central Bank and the pledge to assure unlimited support by the ECB on CEE Euro state members in August 2012 have been turning points in the delicate and complex liquidity transmission mechanism. Though liquidity market normalization is still distant, significant steps forward in recent months, including ECB Long Term Repurchasing Operations, have ensured liquidity to banks and cooled concerns. At least for the time being.

Despite the exceptional environment and events, this book is not a descriptive chronicle of crises and political or monetary fallouts, but rather an attempt to present experiences and indications on liquidity funding risks, starting from a detailed reading and commentary on the bulky and often cumbersome regulatory texts. The reminders and references to regulations are a key driver as they will, in the end, inevitably be dealt with and will constitute compulsory requirements for most banks.

This thread is followed through the first five chapters. The first is meant to present liquidity risk management in current financial markets and banking, with a first indication of how funding liquidity is an increasingly relevant factor to control and manage, together with an overview of regulatory frameworks.

The second chapter focuses on funding liquidity in the shorter maturities, up to one year and mostly within the immediate refinancing time horizons that were so critical during the Lehman crisis and are at the heart of the new regulatory liquidity frameworks. The analysis will touch upon the construction and use of the cash flow ladder, moving on then to the calculation of the liquidity coverage ratio. Related to short-term obligations are the monitoring of specific risk indicators and the intraday liquidity risk, which is particularly important for banks' treasury operations. The analysis concludes with the funding concentration assessment, a necessary component for a complete grasp of exposure and sound funding risk management.

Liquidity risk is also a matter of balance sheet sustainability, and the third chapter touches on structural funding strategies and valuation. It is here introduced as the Net Stable Funding Ratio, with a depositor's modelling overview completing it, essential for any meaningful analysis on funding stability. These are combined with scenario and stress testing, cash horizons and liquidity buffers, included here as components for the structural funding strategy rather than in the short-term section.

Chapter 4 is included mostly for completeness and is a rapid overview of liquidity value at risk models and measurement techniques other than those in Chapters 2 and 3; it should indeed be the subject of a dedicated work and presented here is a compact and essential concept description, distinguishing liquidation adjusted value at risk on the assessment of impact on securities for forced disposal of available amounts and the market liquidity Value at Risk, measuring the VaR for different levels of market depth for different security types.

Chapter 5 looks more at governance rules and processes to adequately control liquidity risks, looking at regulatory indications and providing insights on reporting and control standards, limit setting and contingency planning.

Funding and Market Liquidity

We introduce funding liquidity risk in this first chapter and the stance of some regulators on the controls expected. The first section highlights some facts, events and changes in market conditions that have increased the importance of this risk type, so relevant in recent years. It should also provide an overview of the challenges that banks' treasury functions will face and will suggest how a financial institution could address and possibly manage them, in particular when one is experiencing stressed, difficult market conditions. The second section presents some indications on the management of liquidity funding risk, based on the author's experience and lessons learnt. The third and longest section describes and comments on regulatory frameworks – focusing on the International Basel Committee, EBA, PRA, USA FED – on liquidity and funding liquidity requirements and indications.

1.1 LIQUIDITY IN THE FINANCIAL MARKETS

Like seatides going up and down, the financial markets history shows a recurrence of events and conditions can be seen as recursive. Further, we can see that something influential at times of abundance

1

becomes suddenly crucial and pricey under other market conditions that are stable, and prices that are reliable when the tide goes out could then change substantially as it comes in. So it was, for example, in the money markets and interbank lending, with the exchange of deposits and funds amongst banks and companies, and then across government and countries. The term liquidity risk can refer to different aspects of risk exposure, indeed though generically indicated as liquidity, one has quite a range of exposures. Possibly, the first distinction we want to make is that between trading versus banking book liquidity exposure, the market liquidity risk and funding liquidity risk. We can define market liquidity risk as the impact on the price of an asset when one disposes of it onto the market/liquidates it. The varying market conditions at the moment of the liquidation of that specific asset are commonly addressed as market liquidity risk or liquidity at risk and this is usually an additional risk element of the overall market risk that takes specifically into account the cost of selling or trying to sell the whole stock of a specific asset. It is quantified in terms of changes in the bid-ask spread and asset price itself as a result of the sale. While many markets are very liquid and deep, this is not the case for some securities and markets, and situations vary depending on market conditions as stress market conditions and rating deterioration will have a great impact. Funding liquidity risk is instead conceptually related to the banking book and the bank's capacity to ensure its payment obligations as due contractually. This is also referred to as the refinancing risk (Figure 1.1 below presents the European Central Bank official refinancing rate from March 2008 through March 2013) and it can be divided, in turn, into short-term refinancing – where banks have to meet deadlines in a few days or a few months, sometimes having to ensure balancing of cash inflows and outflows of billions – and that of long-term equilibrium or imbalances in funding maturity profiles and invested assets.

For banks, liquidity represents the capacity to secure the necessary funding, either through attracting deposits – wholesale or

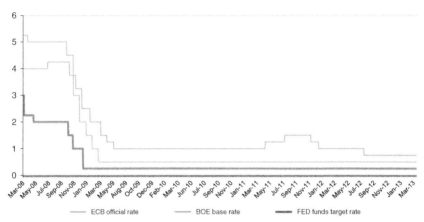

FIGURE 1.1 Central banks' official rates.
Source: ECB, BoE, FED.

individual – or from their own immediately available cash or through pledging unencumbered assets to other financial institutions that can easily be converted into cash in the markets. Banks' current operations also generate income flows that can be considered for liquidity ends, as any means of attracting additional inflows over time can also be considered part of banks' cash sources.

So then, liquidity risk is the diminished capacity to gather cash against payment needs in normal market conditions. The capacity for meeting financing obligations ought to include sudden reductions in funding capacity or unexpected peaks in cash demands. The assets available for funding capacity should be sufficient to offset the net outflow in both normal conditions and during financial market crises; the available counterbalancing capacity is a measure of banks' refinancing, buffers or liquidity reserve that will permit banks to tackle unexpected adverse net cash flows. However, on the government side, systemic risk is the paramount risk; sudden deposit runs and withdrawals may require larger buffers than banks might desire in terms of risk appetite and cost efficiency.

Banks' liquidity buffers encompass cash and securities, kept to sustain liquidity needs in periods of market stress: these consist of cash and other unencumbered stocks and allow them to meet payments in critical market conditions, setting also a target minimum survival period. One should build counterbalancing capacity during normal market conditions, therefore anticipating this complexity when a liquidity crisis heats up is a core part of regular liquidity refinancing and target plans, balancing the cash inflows and outflows to guarantee adequate sources of funding are provided and appropriately used.

Regulators typically address both sides of the balance sheet and the importance of timing: liquidity becomes the ability to make payments as they fall due and to ensure asset growth or lending renewal. More recently, there has been a focus on the negative impact on earnings and capital. Regulators may differentiate between several subsets of liquidity risk depending on the time horizon considered (e.g. strategic vs. tactical), distinguishing between normal and stressed periods (contingency liquidity risk) and types of risks (e.g. funding vs. market liquidity risk).

1.1.1 Definition of funding and liquidity risks

Liquidity risk is the current or prospective risk arising from an institution's inability to meet its liabilities/obligations as they come due without incurring unacceptable losses. This is usually referred to as *funding liquidity risk*. There is also a market dimension to liquidity risk that has become more relevant in recent years as institutions' reliance on market or wholesale funding has increased.

Market liquidity risk is the risk that a position cannot easily be unwound or offset at short notice without significantly influencing the market price, because of inadequate market depth or market disruption.

One way to cover a funding shortfall is through asset sales, here the ability to obtain funds through the sale of assets mitigates funding liquidity risk. Market illiquidity or reduced market liquidity can disrupt an institution's ability to raise cash, and thus its ability to manage its funding liquidity risk.

Expert discussion suggests this definition of market liquidity risk might be considered too narrow, in that the absence of market liquidity to unwind or offset a position, which only affects changes in value, does not impact cash flows. The change in value could result in liquidity demand via margin calls or additional collateral requirements and could be of such a magnitude as to cause a material erosion in the capital strength of the institution and/or a rating downgrade.

Beyond the general definition of liquidity, attention should be paid to the liquidity of each individual asset. The general liquidity squeeze prompted by the Lehman crisis, during which presumed highly liquid assets became completely illiquid for more than six months, calls for fresh contemplation of what constitutes a liquid asset and the definition and application in banks of sound liquidity risk management.

In assessing the liquidity value of liquid assets, the time-to-cash period (the time necessary to convert assets into cash) should be considered. A distinction can be made between assets pledged/deposited at central banks, which can be drawn on immediately, and assets on the balance sheet that may have been pledged as eligible collateral, which may take some time to draw on. The time needed to convert a drawn currency to the currency required should also be considered.

Central banks are an important potential provider of funding through refinancing operations, which are distinct from intraday credit. But institutions do not know in advance how much funding they will receive: they receive only what they are allocated in the auction process. In addition, funds are distributed only once per week. Banks can also draw on central banks' overnight facilities in the course of normal business, but liquidity management should take into account the reputation risk (kind of *stigma*) potentially associated with the possibility of extraordinary drawings.

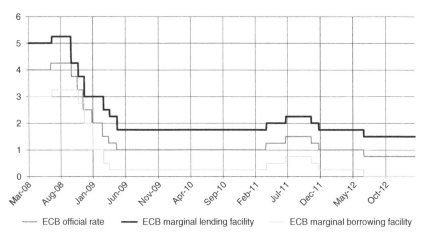

FIGURE 1.2 ECB monetary policy corridor.
Source: ECB.

Thus banks should not rely too heavily on obtaining funding from central banks.

In times of stress, market liquidity may deteriorate. Depending on the type of stress, the deterioration may be specific to certain kinds of assets or it may be more general. The central bank will continue to provide liquidity against eligible assets. When the broader asset market liquidity deteriorates, central bank eligibility may become more important (Figure 1.2 presents the European Central Bank official, lending and borrowing rates from March 2008), as observed during the 2007–08 crisis or the later Greek crisis. Banks may tend to pledge their relatively illiquid assets at central banks, when eligible, in order to use their most liquid/marketable assets to extend their liquidity buffer as much as possible.

Liquid assets are usually defined as assets that can be quickly and easily converted into cash in the market at a reasonable cost. In this respect, due consideration should be made of the time-to-cash period. In order to analyse the liquidity of an asset, institutions and supervisory authorities need to differentiate between normal and stressed times, taking into account the role of central banks' refinancing policies, particularly in times of stress.

Liquidity risk can also be triggered by credit risk, the bank being exposed to the failure of its counterparties and their obligations due; as a counterparty to other market participants it may fail to meet commitments at a reasonable and timely cost, and as a provider of credit it is exposed to liquidity risk linked to the credit quality of its portfolio.

Reputation risk can affect banks' funding capacity; liquidity problems tend to rapidly become visible to the market, seriously damaging reputation or rating.

Market risk, mainly interest rate volatility, drives liquidity risk management and the market value of securities depends on the number of market participants, their size, the frequency of the transactions and assets' ratings. Critical market conditions lead to uncertainty over the value of assets; margin calls on derivatives in such cases also have implications. Large banks also rely on regular functioning of foreign exchange markets, while interruptions in that functioning can trigger liquidity risk.

Concentration may also generate liquidity risk: funding concentration risk emerges when withdrawal of a few liabilities could be significant to the bank's overall funding and difficult to replace in a timely manner. Operational risk coming from payment system disruptions or delays can be very dangerous during severe and prolonged liquidity crises.

A bank should not undertake imprudent liquidity risk management and hold lower levels of liquidity owing to the expectation that central banks will provide support in the event of a market-wide stress and – for firms whose failure might have systemic consequences – firm-specific stress. Although managers and shareholders have strong incentives, arguably without regulation, to build in some resilience to liquidity stress by holding sufficient amounts of liquidity, these incentives may well prove insufficient. This would not be a problem if the consequences of a firm's insufficient resilience to liquidity stress were confined solely to shareholders and managers. But, as recent events have shown, this is not the case.

A bank will remain liquid as long as creditors have confidence in it, and believe other creditors also have confidence. A sudden loss of confidence, whether rational or irrational, will result in liquidity difficulties. We do not consider that holding a buffer of liquid assets designed to protect against liquidity stress is sufficient. Each firm should know its gross liquidity risk, not just the mechanisms to mitigate the risk when crystallized. At all times, we would expect firms to stress test their balance sheets against the stress test scenarios outlined in Chapter 3 and, where any weaknesses are identified, to limit or restrict the impact of the stress. The key is to ensure that the entire liquidity profile of the firm is such that liquidity risk in the firm does not exceed acceptable levels.

History has demonstrated that during a severe liquidity crisis it is the individual position of the various legal entities within a group that matters most. Supervisors, therefore, have to be satisfied with the liquidity position of the locally incorporated entity or local branch. While some major internationally active groups may strongly disagree with this assertion, recent events have clearly shown that internationally active financial groups can default and that, in such an event, local creditors and customers can be significantly disadvantaged.

The market turbulence of the last decade has also demonstrated that many tend to underestimate the potential extremity of liquidity stresses in their stress testing and CFPs. Regulation has to address this potential shortcoming in firms' liquidity risk management approach. This will be of particular importance in the medium- to long-term future, when the effects of the current crisis have abated and the lessons once learned may have been forgotten.

Contrary to widely held assumptions, extreme liquidity events are not all that rare in the global financial markets. While the length and intensity of the current crisis may be unprecedented, name-specific and even wider liquidity events occur with some frequency. As noted above, any crisis of confidence will invariably have certain liquidity implications. It is therefore necessary for our new regime to prepare for the next crisis and ensure that firms' resilience to liquidity stresses remains high, even during business-as-usual periods.

Models have only a limited role to play in liquidity regulation, as liquidity stresses are heterogeneous events that make it difficult to construct meaningful probability distributions. We agree that internal models can play a useful role in a firm's liquidity risk management, however, they are only one of many tools a firm should apply.

1.2 MANAGING LIQUIDITY RISK

Funding liquidity is closely monitored by banking regulators and it is increasingly the focus of internal projects as well as of staff search companies and specialized training firms; it is nowadays considered of strategic importance. It has followed somewhat the same development as the operational risk in banking: once it was considered somehow of lesser importance compared to credit or market risk exposure, then liquidity risk management became a pivotal element of banks' strategic plans, investments and organization. Besides liquidity risk measurement and control, the very change in relevance of such a risk to banks has assured the greatest importance and management role. Banks then need to ensure a comprehensive review and assessment of liquidity risk exposure, control and management processes is in place. An integral element of the overall risk culture framework is ensuring that there is a widespread understanding throughout the organization of liquidity exposure and how this needs to be managed, and how liquidity is specifically reflected in the risk appetite.

1.2.1 Liquidity risk's framework

We should first point out that banks should develop their risk culture through policies, examples, communication and training of staff regarding their responsibilities on risk. Staff should be fully aware of their responsibilities relating to risk management and this should not be confined to risk specialists or control functions. Business units, under the oversight of the management body, should be primarily responsible for managing risks on a day-to-day basis, taking into account the bank risk tolerance/appetite and in line with its policies, procedures and controls.

As repeatedly addressed in previous Basel capital accords, banks should have a risk management framework extending across all their business, support and control units, recognizing fully the economic substance of its risk exposures and encompassing all relevant risks (e.g. financial and non-financial, on and off balance sheet, and whether or not contingent or contractual). Its scope should not be limited to credit, market, liquidity and operational risks, but should also include concentration, reputation, compliance and strategic risks.

The liquidity risk framework should enable the institution to make informed decisions based on information derived from identification, measurement or assessment and monitoring of risks. Risks should be evaluated bottom-up and top-down, through the management chain as well as across business lines, using consistent terminology and compatible methodologies throughout the institution and its group.

The liquidity risk management framework should be subject to independent internal or external review and reassessed regularly against the institution's risk tolerance/appetite, taking into account information from the risk control function and, where relevant, the risk committee. Factors that should be considered include internal and external developments, including balance sheet and revenue growth, increasing complexity of the institution's business, risk profile and operating structure, geographic expansion, mergers and acquisitions and the introduction of new products or business lines. The remuneration policy and practices should be consistent with its risk profile and promote sound and effective risk management. The bank remuneration policy should be coherent with its values, business strategy, risk tolerance/appetite and long-term interests. It should not encourage excessive risk-taking. Guaranteed variable remuneration or severance payments that end up rewarding failure are not consistent with sound risk management nor the pay-for-performance principle and should, as a general rule, be prohibited.

For staff whose professional activities have a material impact on the risk profile of an institution (e.g. management body members, senior management, risk-takers in business units, staff responsible for internal control and any employee receiving total remuneration that takes them into the same remuneration bracket as senior management and risk takers), the remuneration policy should set up specific arrangements to ensure their remuneration is aligned with sound and effective risk management.

It is of the utmost importance that control function staff should be adequately rewarded so as to ensure they fulfil their objectives and that performance is not linked to that of the business they are monitoring. In particular, where a variable component is included, it should relate to that of the overall risk division compensation, while defining individual valuation factors that are not purely economic/results related is also necessary. The performance assessment for bonus/variable pay should include adjustments for the different risks, including that of liquidity risk. The bank's management should be ensured a balanced percentage of basic salary and variable bonus payments. A significant bonus as a percentage of basic salary should not be composed solely of cash but should be flexible and include risk-adjusted weights, while timing of the bonus payment should ensure it considers the bank's risk performance. We should have liquidity funding in the overall risk management framework and this needs to include policies, procedures, limits and controls providing adequate, timely and daily identification. It is necessary to be assessing, monitoring and reporting the risks of the individual desks and business lines as well as the overall exposure. The risk management framework needs to encompass specific guidance on the implementation of strategies, ensuring and maintaining appropriate risk limits given the set risk appetite, available capital base and strategies. The bank aggregate risk exposures should respect these set limits; the bank's management should follow up any relevant breaches of limits and ensure these are escalated and resolved (see Chapter 5).

When we are identifying and measuring risks, we should combine forward and backward looking analysis with the monitoring of daily risk exposures, considering the combination of different risk types and businesses, so as to control concentration exposure. Scenario analysis and stress testing are analyses meant to spot potential risk exposures, while standard historical controls are designed to identify the current risk exposure.

Management decisions on setting the risk limits should not only rely on quantitative information or model outputs, but consider the limitations of metrics and models following a qualitative approach such as expert assessment or an internal analysis. Macroeconomic trends and data are other important factors to include on exposure and portfolio risk assessment, remembering that we also need to base decisions on these analyses.

We need established regular and clear reporting to the senior management, business and other control functions involved: we need to design reports that are distributed in a timely manner, are accurate and highlight the key risk factors, so that management can understand anomalies or jump in exposures and proceed then to the necessary course of action.

We need to bear in mind that the reporting framework isn't just a document for information, it is key evidence for auditors and regulators and the base for presenting and assessing exposure: so management attention and effort must be devoted to its regular preparation and discussion and it needs to represent appropriately the business set-up and its changes over time. We need to ensure the reporting responsibilities are part of dedicated internal policies and there are specific internal procedures. We must also consider report production in the contingency plans. We need to make sure that the bank risk committee receives regular formal reports from the designated risk control functions.

We need a structured liquidity internal control framework, independent from business and risk takers, with appropriate skills, staffing, systems and budget to ensure they comply with responsibilities. The risk control framework should be designed to ensure effective and efficient processes, adequate control of risks in compliance with laws, regulations, supervisory requirements, internal rules and decisions taken. The internal control framework should cover the entire bank and should be tailored to its business structure, with adequate administrative and accounting procedures.

In developing the liquidity internal control framework, we need to outline a clear, transparent and documented decision-making process, setting out responsibilities for implementing internal rules and decisions. In order to implement such a robust liquidity internal control framework in all areas of the institution, the business and support units should be responsible in the first place for setting and maintaining control policies and procedures.

A functioning liquidity internal control framework also requires that an internal audit verifies that these policies and procedures are correctly applied. Second level control functions must not report to the risk-taking functions and also ought to be independent from each other, as are those performing types of control (compliance, audit, risk management). For smaller banks, risk control and compliance functions may be combined.

In setting up the liquidity risk control function, four conditions need to be respected: it must be separate from the activities it is assigned to monitor and control; it should report to a function that has no responsibility for managing the activities it is assigned to monitor and control; it should report directly to the management board; and remuneration of liquidity control staff should not be linked to the performance of the activities that the control function monitors and controls. We need to ensure the liquidity risk control function is adequately staffed in terms of numbers and skills throughout the controlled legal entities that have such exposure. The risk control staff must be regularly trained and have appropriate systems, accessing the data necessary to perform the control tasks.

The liquidity risk control functions should regularly report to the management board and committees on identified weaknesses, and follow up on previous risk management interventions and any recommendations. The liquidity risk control function is ensuring that liquidity risk exposure is identified and properly measured, providing the relevant independent information, analysis and view on the decisions made by the business, checking consistency of the bank's risk appetite, and recommending improvements if deemed necessary.

When banks are large, complex and sophisticated it might be considered valuable to further articulate the liquidity risk control functions; however, it is important that there is an overall central liquidity risk control in charge of providing a consolidated view. The liquidity risk control function needs to be actively involved in elaborating and reviewing the bank's risk strategy and tolerance/appetite levels proposed by business units. Preparing the bank's risk strategy and policy should be done together with the risk officer and business units. The business units should comply with risk limits, liquidity risk control should be responsible for ensuring the limits are in line with the institution's overall risk appetite/risk tolerance and monitoring on an on-going basis that the institution is not taking on excessive risk. Liquidity risk function involvement in the decision-making processes should ensure risk considerations are appropriately considered: responsibility for the decisions taken remains with the risk-taking units and the management board. The liquidity risk function needs to analyse trends and recognize emerging risks arising from market conditions, back-testing risk outcomes against previous estimates to assess and improve the accuracy and effectiveness of the liquidity risk management process. We are also expected to monitor the liquidity exposures in the subsidiaries. The liquidity risk control shall assess limit breaches or rule violation, informing the business units concerned.

1.2.2 Chief Risk Officer's role

The role of the bank's Chief Risk Officer, a role that should be present in all banks as well as the compliance officer and internal audit, is one of exclusive responsibility for monitoring the different risks and the set-up of the risk management framework across the entire organization. The risk officer is in charge of ensuring comprehensive and understandable information on risks, thus enabling the Management Board to understand the bank's overall risk profile, therefore he/she should have sufficient operating experience, independence and seniority to face other senior business managers and have the capacity, if necessary, to challenge or halt decisions that could negatively affect the bank. The risk officer and the Management Board (or relevant committees) are expected to discuss key risk issues, including developments that may be diverging from set risk tolerance/appetite and strategy.

When the risk officer has the right to veto decisions, we should include within internal risk the circumstances in which the risk officer is authorized to do this (e.g. a credit or investment decision or the setting of a limit), indicating escalation procedures and Management Board involvement. If the bank does not assign such responsibility to the CRO, such a function must be assigned to another senior officer, provided there is no conflict of interest. We need internal processes in place to assign the position of the risk officer and to withdraw his or her responsibilities, and if the CRO is replaced it should be done with the prior approval of the Management Board.

1.3 REGULATORY FRAMEWORKS

In December 2010 the Basel Committee on Banking Supervision issued a new set of rules specifically designed to normalize liquidity risk management in banks following the Lehman crisis and troubles experienced then. This detailed set of rules, commonly referred to as the third Basel capital accord or Basel 3, follows a previous recommendations document – the sound principles for sound liquidity risk management, published in 2008 – where the Committee indicated principles on management and control processes. The two sets are meant to be integrated and their guidelines applied by banks to liquidity risk management. The December 2010 standards address two requirements: short-term liquidity refinancing to guarantee bank survival in the case of very tense market conditions and a long-term funding balance to ensure sustainable balance sheet financing. The intention of the Basel Committee is that such liquidity control standards should be adopted by national regulators and compelled in financial institutions by January 2015 at the latest for short-term liquidity and January 2018 for long-term structural funding. Discussions are still taking place and final requirements or deadlines for adoption may vary.

Basel 3's short-term liquidity requirements assess and strengthen banks' survival capacity, checking the drain of funding under stressed market conditions and imposing stocks of assets to counterbalance such adverse conditions. The target is building a buffer of assets, mostly securities, available for sale or refinancing and always in the hands of the bank's treasury to meet contractual set payments for a period of 30 calendar days. The rationale of Basel 3 for setting this to one month is based on the belief that a national bank, financial authorities and the bank's management will then have sufficient time available to find means to meet their obligations. Whether this is a sound estimate is one of the points this book will address, articulated specifically in Chapter 4. The liquidity cover ratio, LCR, results from the bank's high quality liquid assets (see later) over the total net cash outflows on the following 30 calendar days and it is set to be always at least greater than one (namely stock high quality assets/net cash outflows over 30 days).

The Basel Committee provides some minimum standards: rather than being prescriptive and supplying parameters and detailed approaches, the preferred approach – as in previous Basel requirements – has been more focused on the principles and drivers banks

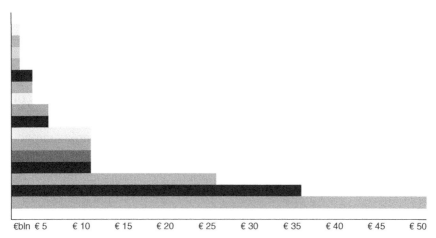

FIGURE 1.3 EU gross liquidity shortfall. Each line represents a country. *Source:* EBA voluntary LCR monitoring exercise.

should follow. This has been the common approach as the Basel rules are supranational and will have to be implemented and national rules issued that provide more detailed indications. In any case, the indications listed before for stress testing are considered a base scenario, banks are not only entitled but encouraged to further analyse and develop their own scenarios and hypotheses, as that in Basel mostly summarizes lessons learnt during market liquidity crises. The objective of the new ratio requirement is to ensure that banks, even in extremely penalizing market liquidity conditions, have 30 working days' survival, especially the large, systemic international banks, so allowing sufficient time for intervention and hopefully avoiding contagion (see Figure 1.3 showing the results of an EBA voluntary exercise on potential LCR requirements' liquidity shortfall for different EU countries).

A fundamental element of all the regulation and the core of the debate between banking industry representatives and financial regulators is the stock of securities and cash that banks ought to keep at any time available for refinancing. Clearly the debate focuses on the amount: banks do not like the idea of being forced to keep low yield, large portfolios of securities at all times. Regulators would instead favour large portfolios of bonds and cash, unpledged, to face potential shortcomings in funding. Other than a matter of capital standards and deposits assurance, there is a strong debate on the banks' profitability and therefore economic sustainability. Large portfolios of unsecured bonds will not only reduce profitability if these are of the highest rating. They will also significantly reduce the bank's capacity to finance companies and private customers, hindering growth in times of crisis. Holding liquid assets and securities defined as *high quality* (see Chapters 2 and 3 for an extensive list and description), presents tradeoffs and I do not believe it is the solution to liquidity crises: such assets experience varying prices and dynamics if we look at US treasuries or German bunds, and these move at different times following political and economic speculations and expectations that then change substantially, even reverting valuation extremely quickly. An interesting example in this regard is the fluctuations since 2008 of gold prices, reaching an all-time peak during the Greek and Italian crisis when the market feared European Union breakdown, to post-August 2012 stability and then rapid decline: discussions have taken place over the rationales, however the regulators' inclination to assume gold is the safest and most liquid asset type for liquidity refinancing at times of crisis might be correct in some circumstances but prove untrue if situations vary, as just presented. I am therefore of the opinion that the Basel 3 prescriptions on high liquid stock need further analysis and that banks are more likely to cope well at times of crisis with well-managed processes, credit underwriting and careful strategic planning of their funding needs rather than by increasing their holding of large quantities of AAA rated bonds.

In Chapters 2 and 3 we will outline the LCR and net stable funding ratio components and their calculation. In the first section I will focus on the main rationales underlying the liquidity regulatory framework: strengthening the banks' available resource to withstand market turbulence and unexpected liquidity needs. Securities of the

TABLE 1.1 The new Basel liquidity regulatory framework application phases.

	1 January 2015	1 January 2016	1 January 2017	1 January 2018	1 January 2019
min LCR	60%	70%	80%	90%	100%

Source: Basel Committee on Banking Supervision.

highest standing and liquidity are intended for pledging and to ensure collateral facilities: in cases of their simultaneous disposal by many banks, even the highest rated have incurred price decline and could even actually collapse if there was a definite attempt to dispose of large quantities and there were no buyers. Thus, the actual objective is ensuring refinancing, rather than selling securities in the market. The crisis in Europe presented a situation where banks simply stopped lending to each other even against highly rated pledged bonds and preferred using these for central bank facilities. Then it was up to the European Central Bank to ensure money market transmission and it was through this rather than normal interbank lending that liquidity flows were ensured. It is therefore an element to consider that holding the lowest yielding, highest rated securities is not going to change the way banks ensure liquidity in stressed conditions, this being through the central bank. There, the haircuts applied to higher or lower rated securities were an issue and hampered financing capacity; but it was through large refinancing operations that the falling prices of some government bonds and higher haircuts were, in the end, resolved. Table 1.1 shows the new Basel liquidity framework implementation schedule for the Liquidity Coverage Ratio.

The regulators found out that the event triggering Lehman's default was an intraday liquidity drain and the bank's management failing to regularly and timely verify funds available net of those pledged either in repos or as trade collateral. *Unencumbered* means not used to secure explicitly or implicitly other transactions (e.g. derivatives, repos, loans). The securities that the bank receives in reverse repo and securities financing transactions that are deposited at the bank and are available contractually to be reused can also be practically part of the stock and can be added to own funds. Supervisors, looking at the dynamic of the Lehman crisis, discovered that another problem was the unclear attribution of securities for pledging to trading rather than for banking book payment flows netting: at a time of difficulty this proved another dangerous element for timely risk management intervention. So we should keep a stock of liquid assets dedicated to payments on banking books and customer deposits neatly separated from those securities assigned and used for trading position collateral management: the bank's counterbalancing capacity must be separated, clearly identified, monitored through daily reporting and should be strategically managed as the bank's source of emergency or contingent liquidity (Figure 1.4 reports the available high quality liquid assets that would become eligible for counterbalancing with the introduction of the LCR, based on a sample of 357 banks).

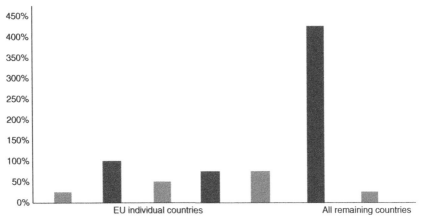

FIGURE 1.4 Banks' volume of high quality liquid assets eligible by introduction of LCR as a percentage of gross liquidity shortfall, single bars referring to an individual country.
Source: EBA voluntary LCR monitoring exercise.

I want to mention here another issue regarding a bank's available securities for refinancing: regulators are indicating that client securities that have been used by the bank, typically against a fee, for money market liquidity, cannot be included in the official counterbalancing capacity stock. The point is clear: banks should not arbitrage and transform clients' funds to offset regulatory requirements. On the other hand, offering such an option to retail brokerage clients can be handy and prove convenient for the bank and its customer: here risk management must be aware of the potential risk and must assess the size and types of securities targeted, together with the necessary compliance function valuation. The possibility of exposing the bank's customer to unwanted or unclearly disclosed risks must be carefully understood and monitored.

1.3.1 Total net cash outflows

The term total net cash outflows – the payments made and received – is another pillar of the liquidity risk assessment in regulatory frameworks. In the Basel 3 approach, the payments received and obligations need to be projected for the following 30 calendar days, applying predetermined stressed assumptions to verify the potential impact and available resources to fund unexpected gaps; while the total expected cash outflows are calculated by multiplying the outstanding balances of various categories or types of liabilities and off-balance-sheet commitments by the rates at which these are expected to be withdrawn as the total expected cash inflows are determined, multiplying the outstanding balances of various receivables by the rates at which they are expected to flow in, with a set cap on total expected cash outflows (total net cash outflows over the next 30 calendar days are calculated as *outflows – minimum (inflows; set outflows %)*). We need to carefully verify the correct assignments of cash flows to time buckets and apply consistent rules for mapping into limited granular time sets, checking also that these are standard across the different business lines and data sources (we need to take into account that roll-off, draw-down rates and similar factors will be identical across countries as per the Basel 3 accord; some parameters can be set by national regulators).

1.3.2 Long-term funding requirements

In the Basel 3 requirements there is a specific one on maintaining the bank's long-term balance of maturing assets and funding liability, with the objective of ensuring that the banks are best prepared to tackle stressed market conditions. The metric hinges on a minimal acceptable amount of stable funding based on the characteristics of assets for maturity over one year, the separation point of LCR and NSFR measurements. The latter, or net stable funding ratio, is the other side of the coverage ratio and completes the quantitative requisites for banks' funding liquidity.

In general, wholesale banks approach the balance sheet maturity transformation as an integral part of their business. The medium long-term standard is designed to ensure that long-term assets are funded with a core set of similar longer term liabilities to ensure balance. We will discuss again the problem of imposing such a strict balance on banks' profitability further on: the financial industry's worried reaction towards a strict application of the medium long-term balance is driven by profitability concerns, especially during economic recessions, low interest rates and many banks going through heavy deleveraging asset programmes, such that it will be uncertain and very difficult to ensure a stable and profitable credit spread from companies and retail customer financing and at the same time balance these with maturing financing liabilities.

The long-term ratio hinges on the net liquid asset and cash capital methodologies used widely by international banks, equity analysts and rating agencies. In computing the amount of assets that should be backed by stable funding, the ratio calculation encompasses the estimated stable funding for all assets and securities on banks' balance sheets. This should be carried out irrespective of the accounting classification of assets into trading or available-for-sale or held-to-maturity. The stable funding sources to be considered for the ratio are also intended to be held for potential liquidity requirements deriving also from off-balance-sheet posts. The long-term ratio is thus the amount of stable funding for assets maturing in the longer term and ought to be greater than one: funding considered stable is considered to be the amount of equity and liability financing assumed to remain as sources of funding over a one-year time horizon and primarily in stressed market conditions; the amount needed to ensure stability for asset financing will vary according to the types of assets including off-balance-sheet exposures and changes in the combination of the two.

1.3.3 Banks' funding

A number of market developments have created new challenges for banks, like the increasing reliance on market funding and the use of complex financial instruments, combined with the globalization of financial markets. More recently, large banks have shifted from deposit-based funding to market funding sources, the originate-to-distribute model: supporting banks managing new challenges like the decline in the retail deposit base (especially long-term deposits) and more volatile retail customer tendencies, it has increased reliance on market sources of funding – banks are originating and underwriting credit assets and distributing them to various types of investors through syndication, securitization and credit derivatives.

We know that retail deposit funding is relatively stable and presents lower credit and interest rate sensitivity than other funding sources. So the bank's higher use of market funding sources leads to a higher exposure to price and credit sensitivities for major fund providers, like wholesale certificates of deposit. As the wholesale funding pricing also tends to be more expensive than retail deposit funding, this change will likely reduce the bank's profitability: most wholesale funding needs to be rolled over frequently, often daily, and it is therefore exposed to changes in the funding liquidity conditions. The increasing share of interbank exposures and money market instruments in banks' funding can provide an additional source of liquidity risk. We are now aware that in times of stress reliance on the full functioning and liquidity of financial markets may not be correct, and those banks that rely heavily on wholesale funding, securitization or have significant contingent liquidity commitments (e.g. conduits) will mostly be affected.

Based on experience we know that funding liquidity can be driven by factors such as:

- The shortening of maturity in the interbank market, where the borrowing gradually reduces to overnight or just a few days.
- A marked shift towards secured lending such as repos (i.e. reduced unsecured lending) and cancellation of committed liquidity lines by other wholesale banks.
- Reduced CDs and CPs funding market.
- ABS markets disappearing, irrespective of the issuer rating, therefore reducing funding through securitization and impacting greatly on SPV or conduit funding.
- Hampered issuance of medium- and long-term bonds.
- A decrease in liquidity on cross-currency swap markets also in some major currencies (USA dollar, Euro).

These elements are typically also leading to an increase in the cost of funding, and when there is an over-dependence on wholesale funding this can lead to a great liquidity problem (e.g. Northern Rock bank).

We note that the originate-to-distribute model has increased banks' dependence on capital markets as the global financial system increases the risk of a domino effect to the whole market. As cost and availability of unsecured lending depends firstly on a bank's credit quality/rating, if it incurs significant losses (and these are publicly known) then the bank might also struggle to obtain funding at acceptable cost, unless posting guarantees.

The use of complex financial derivatives is also exposing banks to additional complex liquidity risk forms; where we need assessment and understanding of whether the underlying liquidity of the market will bear market stress conditions, mark-to-market values of the positions may be difficult to determine during liquidity crises, likely leading to additional funding requirements:

- Mark-to-market losses will affect earnings and the capital base, then hampering access to unsecured credit markets possibly only at higher prices, again further affecting earnings and capital.
- Adverse changes in mark-to-market positions, either from a change in the value of the trading position or a decline in the collateral, will result in additional margin calls.

In general, as complex products can be illiquid and prices difficult to determine (e.g. see IFRS 13 Level 3 Fair Value Adjustments rules) and given that valuation depends on data-intensive statistical models and on scenario analysis, these will generate a greater model risk meant as the possibility of errors in evaluating and pricing the position. For example, an asset can be difficult to value if it is based on dynamic parameters that can change with market conditions or for which no external data are available. Market illiquidity generates additional risk types, like the so-called warehouse risk when the bank is unable to find buyers and is then forced to keep positions: in these circumstances, if the bank does not have sufficient available assets, it will have to post a greater amount of collateral in order to get additional funding sources, while additional asset pledging to get more funding will decrease financial flexibility and affect its credit standing. In the case, for example, of structured securities, it is difficult to forecast how the cash flows generated might behave during market stress, as these are not actively traded and price transparency is limited. Wider bid-ask spreads due to thin trading volumes and the potential for sharp swings in demand can significantly increase their liquidity risk, while for off-balance-sheet obligations this could result in price volatility and liquidity risk in other circumstances. Derivatives and complex financial products pose significant challenges in terms of funding liquidity and should therefore be treated with extreme caution, taking the interlink between the different risk types they generate.

1.3.4 Funding through securitization

While traditional securitization allows banks to get liquidity from previously illiquid assets (such as mortgage or loan portfolios), it also makes them more reliant on the smooth functioning and stability of financial markets. If the liquidity in the securitization market disappears, one could expect some cascade effects; the originating bank will be left with a sudden funding need – and during the crisis some were forced to defer some securitization, so resulting in asset stocks needing to be financed. It is common to first fund the lending book with short-term funding and then replace shorter-term funding with securitizations; if this funding market vanishes, short-term funding will have to be rolled, thus increasing the funding liquidity risk exposure.

All types of securitization also entail contingent liquidity risk, this being the possibility that we might have to ensure liquidity suddenly and likely at a time when it is already harder to access the market. Banks offer liquidity facilities to ensure timely payment of principal and interest if certain set conditions occur (e.g. in the case of a rating downgrade). Some banks have faced additional liquidity calls to support off-balance-sheet investments, as not providing such support would damage their reputation and, in turn, affect their funding capacity (this is discussed at length throughout the book). When the securitized assets are long-term assets, such as residential mortgages, and we are exposed to roll-over risk or the assets are taken back on the balance sheet, this will deteriorate the bank maturity mismatch and short-term funding may come at a higher price. If the overall credit rating deteriorates, or the market illiquidity condition deteriorates, or the liquidity requirements are urgent, we may be pushed to sell assets at then market prices, affecting earnings. Considering that own asset securitization has considerably high origination and management costs and that it is quite a regular funding source for companies, then it may be from here that significant liquidity problems are triggered, especially when there is financial market volatility; securitizations can also generate unexpected outflows when they are required to ensure liquidity to meet contractual commitments.

Linked to securitization are the covenants, the legal clauses relating to specific financial conditions or events that affect the terms of a contract. Financial covenants are commonly included in financial contracts to protect creditors. If the conditions are met, the creditors are allowed to waive the normal terms of the contract on a discretionary basis. In such cases they may require, for example, ending the contract or some other contractually specified action or consequence – such as the posting of additional collateral or a step-up in the interest rate. Covenants can be regarded as a kind of purchased trigger option for the creditors, as they give them a discretionary contingent right. Typical financial covenants included in corporate loan contracts give institutions contingent rights without increasing their liquidity risk. It is not only the covenants included in complex financial instruments used for innovative funding structures that raise liquidity risk management issues, especially during times of stress. For example, various kinds of market adverse condition clauses in securitization contracts contain downgrade triggers and performance triggers (relating to recourse provisions leading to early amortization) that can impose collateral requirements. Drawings on liquidity back-up facilities provided to conduits are based on trigger covenants included in the contracts, and additional collateral requirements could be based on sponsor-linked rating triggers in the context of credit enhancement. The liquidity risk posed by this kind of covenant is often of a low probability–high impact nature. Various triggers can have a substantial liquidity impact, due to extended back-up facilities, early termination/buy-backs, or collateral requirements or margin calls in cash. Even when the conditions of covenants are not fully met, an institution may be forced to buy back assets because of reputation risk. Active management of this reputation risk may avoid additional liquidity risk. Documentation risk can be an element in the liquidity risk of covenants if a dispute arises due to unclear covenant language, for example regarding received liquidity facilities. Due to the limited information available, business activities using complex financial instruments with low probability/high impact liquidity risk may not be visible to the treasury function and thus may not be included in liquidity plans and stress tests. In securitization documents, covenants link to regulatory actions or breaches of thresholds – for example, providing that such actions or breaches trigger early amortization – and could undermine the objectives of those supervisory actions and thresholds. Early amortization can exacerbate liquidity and earnings problems as well as collateral demands and margin calls: for large positions, this may lead to disposal and then impact market liquidity, affecting prices and, in turn, affecting funding capacity for all market participants using the same collateral.

1.3.5 Behavioural changes of customers or investors

Several changes can be observed in retail customers' responses. First, there has been a long-term change from bank deposits to investment or pension funds; this determined deposit bases that were not following loan dynamics, leading to alternative funding sources for banks. There is also a trend of higher price sensitivity and awareness, higher volatility of retail deposits, weaker relevance of the customer relationship, and an increased importance of electronic banking. Many direct obstacles to possibly more volatile cross-border investments, such as restrictions on foreign purchases of domestic assets and limitations on the ability of domestic residents to invest abroad, have been contained: indirect obstacles to cross-border flows – such as high costs of foreign transactions, inadequate information on foreign investments, linguistic obstacles – declined significantly, diminishing the habit of holding on to domestic savings. Another new challenge to liquidity risk management is the uncertainty regarding the degree of commitment to the market of increasingly active unregulated providers of liquidity. There are also doubts over the willingness to invest in credit derivatives and over structured products, such as hedge funds, holding on to their investments in adverse market conditions.

1.3.6 Payment systems

Payment settlement systems process a large part of banks' liquidity flows and have a fundamental role in ensuring smooth functioning of financial markets; their importance has increased with globalization, European integration and Asian countries' greater relevance in the world economy. For liquidity purposes, it becomes clear that regular functioning of these systems is essential to ensure there are no impacts on financial markets and the banks. Larger value payment systems settle predominantly in real time gross settlement, while retail payment systems instead apply net settlement: technological improvements have allowed net settlement systems to become faster and very reliable, decreasing the time for netting and becoming very close to a real-time payment, combined with a reduction and improved efficiency in the collateral posting when gross settlement applies. There has been a move from net towards real-time mechanisms, supported by regulators as gross models are less exposed to systemic risk. Netting reduces credit and liquidity risk, including intraday liquidity requirements, as it lowers the positions held with other banks to a net position, it also has a positive impact on necessary capital. Close-out netting settles with one single payment all claims for the counterparties subject to the netting: these are made on the occurrence of a defined event (e.g. insolvency). We should verify that close-out netting arrangements are legally recognized. We also need to remember that settlement is completed only at the end of day and we should consider payments final only then: if a bank does not ensure payment, other payment orders could be closed with other banks being, in turn, affected. If we are using netting arrangements to mitigate risks, institutions should consider and take into account legal and operational elements to ensure that liquidity risk is measured. Banks use several payment systems, increasing the complexity in intraday payment management as net payment systems need collateral posting to ensure transaction processing. In the case of gross settlement systems, individual payments are processed one by one, thereby containing the settlement risk. We are required to post ensured adequate intraday funds for the smooth processing of transactions. In addition we can use intraday credit facilities, monitoring collateral availability during the day. Trade settlement requires banks to provide funds and collateral as per set contractual agreements and banks' internal functions must verify that contractual requirements are well understood and monitored, and that the correct calculation of margins and collateral requirements are performed.

1.3.7 Correspondent and custody activities

Correspondent banking also funnels payment flows, in particular for intraday liquidity risk, as the collateral posting in terms of securities and/or cash through the corresponding banking may determine the provision as part of the intraday settlement of transactions and it can determine an increase in the intraday exposure. Liquidity exposure will depend on transaction type, securities available for posting and time of day, credit facilities and counterparty rating of those involved. It is important that we control intraday payments carried out through correspondent and custody, looking in particular at the concentration: unexpected changes in payment flows can trigger a domino effect on cash or collateral posting or credit facility use, affecting the correspondent or custodian exposure. Transactions in foreign currencies are typically processed through CLS clearing payment, settling individual payment against others and allowing limits to liquidity risk, especially in foreign currencies. As several foreign exchange trades are settled through correspondent banking, liquidity risk can be contained by the CLS settlement system. We must be aware of the payment systems we are using and their functioning; we should also identify indicators to spot anomalies and duly intervene to avoid correspondence banking impacting our cash flows and liquidity position.

1.3.8 Accounting treatment and liquidity

According to international accounting standards (IFRS), financial assets and liabilities can be classified as held for trading when these are kept for speculation; we can also keep assets to maturity (Hold to Maturity) when we intend to keep them until their contractual expirations and these will then be valued at amortized historical cost.

These classifications for securities are also linked to their liquidity purposes: if we classify a security as H-t-M, it cannot be sold for liquidity purposes (only in specific exception cases, however it can be pledged as collateral for repo transactions. Irrespective of how banks classify securities for accounting purposes, the level of liquidity will still be driven by accounting classification but on financial market valuations. There may be some negative liquidity impact if assets are held in the H-t-M or as loans and receivables but this impact is not that significant.

1.3.9 Diversification of funding sources

Funding concentration materializes when we are overly reliant on one or few funding sources, either a customer or a preferred liquidity channel. Liquidity funding concentration depends on risk appetite and the bank's funding mix. We can define funding concentration as the fund amount that, if withdrawn, would force structural changes in the funding sources. Liquidity funding concentrations typically include:

- Dependence on a restricted number of interbank market providers or large corporate customers.
- Concentration on specific funding purposes.
- Funding concentrations on certain maturity.
- Focus on secured funding.
- Geographical or currency concentrations.

1.3.10 Rating agency approaches to internal methodologies

Broadly speaking, liquidity risk is not a significant determinant of ratings, in comparison with other factors such as profitability and capital. This is especially the case for the largest banks, where the probability of liquidity problems arising is relatively low because of the quality of the banks' risk management systems and their low potential for solvency concerns, which can be a leading indicator of liquidity problems. The methods used by different rating agencies to assess liquidity risk can be quite diverse. The most common quantitative test applied by rating agencies is the assessment of how long a bank could survive without access to market funding; rating agencies allow banks to benchmark against their peers specifically on their liquidity risk systems.

1.3.11 Transparency to the market

We need to pay great attention to the level of disclosure on liquidity risk, taking into account the fact that the bank's reputation is critical to market funding and the funding costs: disclosure to the market becomes crucial. For accounting purposes (IFRS 7), financial liabilities must be disclosed by contractual maturity, undiscounted cash flows and managerial available data. For derivatives, IFRS 7 indicates net amounts should be presented for pay float/receive fixed interest rate swaps for each contractual maturity category when only a net cash flow will be exchanged; a currency swap would need to be included in the maturity analysis using gross cash flows. Investors, customers, depositors and regulators need to be informed of the bank's liquidity risk, as well as the liquidity risk exposures or liquidity buffers.

There is no question of the need for qualitative indications on banks' liquidity risk management: specifically on internal governance and the policies and procedures for managing liquidity risk, a description of systems available and liquidity controls in place. This will help assess the capacity to manage liquidity.

1.3.12 Contingency plans

It is important to have dedicated policies and procedures in place for crisis management, in particular the existence of appropriate stress tests, the composition and robustness of liquidity buffers, and the effectiveness of contingency funding plans. One should check that robust and well-documented stress tests are in place, that their results trigger action and that the assumptions used are appropriate, conservative and regularly reviewed.

Regulators may regard quantitative requirements as a first step and integrate them within the qualitative part of their regime. Other supervisors consider that beyond a certain level of complexity the quantitative approach is less useful in assessing the level of liquidity risk and the quality of risk management than information defined on a case-by-case basis. These allow internal methodologies to replace quantitative requirements at some institutions. Prior to granting any form of recognition to internal methodologies in their approaches, they will assess them and gather supporting evidence that will give them the necessary assurances as to their adequacy.

Regardless of whether internal methodologies are subject to formal approval, assessment will cover:

- Governance, the definition of liquidity risk, risk strategy, involvement of senior management, organizational embedding of liquidity risk management, the structure of limits, interaction with other risks, reporting.
- Sound methodology, useful ratios in assessing the short-term and structural liquidity position of institutions, the composition of the liquidity buffer and the assumptions used, the definition of material cash flows, diversification strategy, internal validation of outcomes, consideration of off-balance-sheet positions, new product process, and the design and embedding of stress tests.
- Conservatism, the use of sufficiently conservative assumptions in calculating ratios.
- Completeness, internal methodologies sufficiently covering the institution's scope of consolidation, and ratios sufficiently covering all material anticipated and unanticipated future inflows and outflows of cash and liquid assets.
- Timeliness of the liquidity overview: data refreshing requirements, sufficiently high frequency of calculation of the ratios.
- Use test, institutions should actually use ratios in their liquidity management.
- Liquidity crisis planning: the contents of the contingency plan, time horizon, strategy for selling assets.
- Cross-border aspects of liquidity management: centralization vs. decentralization, cross-currency liquidity risk management.

Ratios should be useful for assessing both the individual and the aggregate liquidity position in the most important currencies. When using internal methodologies for supervisory purposes, supervisors should assess the adequacy of governance, the soundness of methodologies – including their conservatism and completeness – the timeliness of reviews, the robustness of stress testing, and resilience to liquidity crisis, taking into account external constraints on the transferability of liquidity and the convertibility of currencies. Regulators could explore the possibility of developing a minimum set of common reporting requirements, applicable to all credit institutions and possibly to investment firms that are not restricted to activities on behalf of third parties.

CHAPTER 2

Short-Term Funding

Funding liquidity risk differs at a glance from the more generic liquidity risk, for it is intended as a measurement of immediate survival risk, the possibility that in the days or weeks to come a company might fail in its financial payment obligations. It is a kind of binary risk, and is mostly focused on the closest time maturities. This chapter is thus central for understanding and assessing funding liquidity risk. It presents the cash flow ladder, the survival method applied by treasuries to check inflows and outflows. It moves on to Basel 3's Liquidity Coverage Ratio analysis, also meant for shortest term control. Then, different indicators or sensors of liquidity are presented, taken from internal and external market sources, aiming to measure the temperature of funding liquidity and possibly anticipate anomalies and future difficulties in refinancing. Such exposures are mostly driven by intraday payment flows, and this is covered in a dedicated section. This chapter on funding liquidity risk management closes with an analysis of sources of liquidity and their concentration.

2.1 CASH FLOW LADDER

Liquidity risk measurement can be split into two components: the short-term one for refinancing contractual obligations up to one year and which is focused on the most immediate of those – overnight, one week or 30 days, or two or three months – is the focus of this chapter as the risk measurement methodologies differ substantially from those for long-term liquidity, discussed in Chapter 3. The long-term liquidity risk must consider and measure the sustainability of a bank over a longer time frame of five to ten years, thus giving consideration and actions a more strategic stance. Short-term liquidity risk of up to one year and mostly focusing on three months will deal with the immediate necessity of raising funds to meet contractual obligations maturing in such limited time available and typically will require the warehousing of securities or of other emergency funding.

Cash flows are therefore crucial to control and manage short-term liquidity risk. Contractual maturity mismatch identifies the gaps between the contractual inflows and outflows of liquidity for given time bands. The maturity gaps indicate how much liquidity a bank would have to ensure in each of these time bands if all outflows occurred at the earliest possible date. In managing short-term liquidity risk, commonly a bank treasury uses the cash flow ladder, or just simply the liquidity ladder (see Figure 2.1), where contractual cash and security inflows and outflows from on- and off-balance-sheet items are mapped to set time buckets.

Some indications of the ladder components are provided in the new Basel accord and other regulatory documents, as presented in Chapter 1. There isn't a definitive structure and methodology, however some core elements are the same and are held in common among different approaches. Given the scope of the short-term ladder to allow treasury and risk management a view on the next payments due or expected, in order to address adequate funding needs our approach is to identify all the key elements one needs to take into account; thus, we present and describe how to model:

1. Contractual maturing obligations, in and out cash flows.
2. Rules for mapping flows on the maturity ladder.
3. Flows without contractual certainty.

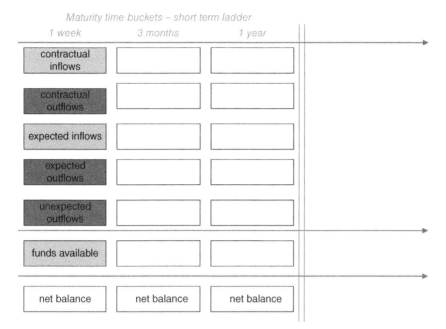

FIGURE 2.1 Liquidity ladder structure.
Source: The author.

4. Unexpected cash flows.
5. Funds available for refinancing.
6. Fund transferability.
7. Total ladder construction.

The short-term ladder components are presented in Figure 2.1. I suggest that the cash flow ladder should be updated at least daily, possibly at same-day closing. Intraday updates may be beneficial, especially in difficult market conditions.

A bank should report contractual cash and security flows in the relevant time buckets based on residual contractual maturity. A more articulated and detailed time bucket structure will provide a precise cash flow position; given the daily or intraday monitoring required by the treasury, one should have a granular representation for the closest maturity (one or two weeks). A detailed interval structure up to one year, updated daily, will be important for monitoring and managing flow dynamics. One could possibly include cash flows for overnight and for each day until the end of the week, then two weeks and monthly to half year; then a quarterly bucketing would be sufficient.

Instruments that have no specific maturity, such as share capital, should be reported separately, with details on the instruments and no assumptions applied to maturity. Information on possible cash flows arising from derivatives such as interest rate swaps and options should also be included to the extent that their contractual maturities are relevant. Some additional accounting information, such as capital or non-performing loans, may be reported separately. An exemplificative ladder is presented in Table 2.1.

2.1.1 Contractual cash flows

Contractual cash flow mapping rules are the foundations of the ladder, whether assumptions of rollover are accepted or hindered (Basel 3 proposals allow liability but hamper the assets, therefore considering term deposits beneficial and renewal of financing uncertain).

Contingent liability exposures – such as contracts with triggers based on a change in price of financial instruments or a downgrade in credit rating – need to be individually assessed. The cash flow ladder is preferably built on contractual maturities for operative reasons, so the treasury can precisely manage funding. Contractual maturity mismatches do not capture outflows that a bank may make in order to protect its franchise, even where contractually there is no obligation to do so. Banks should conduct their own maturity mismatch analyses, based on assumptions of the inflows and outflows of funds in both normal and stress conditions.

When there are material changes to the company or to the business models, it is crucial to forecast cash flow reports as part of the assessment (i.e. in the case of major acquisitions or mergers or the launch of new products).

TABLE 2.1 Mapping cash flows into the liquidity ladder.
Data in millions – imaginary Bank Alpha

	T+1	T+2	1W	2W	1M	2M	3M	4M	5M	6M	12M
Primary Gap	2.82	3.80	−0.25	−9.18	−27.30	−37.82	−42.51	−43.77	−42.02	−42.68	−45.41
Eligible Securities	55.02	53.17	55.13	55.38	64.14	64.26	66.18	65.84	63.54	61.95	48.64
Marketable Securities	8.22	7.94	8.24	8.28	9.58	9.60	9.89	9.84	9.49	9.26	7.27
Cumulative Gap	**66.07**	**64.91**	**63.11**	**54.48**	**46.42**	**36.05**	**33.56**	**31.90**	**31.01**	**28.53**	**10.50**

Source: The author.

2.1.2 Rules for mapping flows on the maturity ladder

The ladder will have a substantially different shape depending on the set time buckets' granularity. For funding liquidity, greater attention should be paid to the closest deadlines, such as overnight and one day to one week. We might find it useful to maintain such a daily breakdown for ten working days and then move onto a week to one month, and from then onwards have a monthly bucket ladder. Indications have been given by regulators and most banks tend to follow a ladder with buckets daily to one week, then on to a monthly one until three months, and from there quarterly until one year – considered the separating point of short to medium long-term funding profiles. Such a decision is often driven by data availability, as per the representation this is also a matter of managerial needs: so whether one keeps a monthly deadline to one year or quarterly will not make a great difference. I prefer and suggest a daily bucket until ten working days and then monthly until eighteen months: this way the rollout dynamic is easier to monitor. One important aspect is the flow mapping when this falls between set time buckets: as an interpolation will not be needed for short-term funding risk control and management, unlike interest rate risk sensitivity, we can follow the rule of assigning the flow to the nearest next maturity interval in full.

2.1.3 Flows without contractual certainty

In banks there are flows with contractual maturity, such as term deposits or repos, addressed in previous sections. There are also cash flows that will occur with certainty and need the bank's timely forecast and planning (e.g. tax payments, predictable but not easily allowing a certain ex/ante flow placing in the ladder). For such flows, a model predicting time and amounts, based on historical and empirical data evidence, is useful and should be applied to include the flows in the ladder.

Rollout assumptions should also be assessed and considered carefully: in the Basel 3 proposal these are explicitly hindered, meaning that the patter or experienced trend or verbal indications that a customer will renew the obligation or a deposit should be considered part of the rollover assumptions, but the contractual maturity should prevail. This is understandable, especially in difficult market conditions and should be seen as a prudential approach. Still, case-by-case analysis and sharing with management and regulators may lead to different choices and result in a different representation of the ladder.

As for so-called commercial network transactions – the retail and corporate network loans and deposit flows – these should be kept separate from the wholesale ladder cash flows as they do not necessarily imply fund transfers, and are then captured in the net commercial deposits balance at the end of the day in the banks' treasury evidence, and as such are reported in the short-term ladder. The principle here is keeping separate the sure cash in/out flows that the bank's treasury must manage, from the account booking of the commercial branch networks and the ongoing customer deposit changes (new, rebated, renewed loans) and banks' treasury cumulative flows that are to be included in the ladder. Rather different will be the cases of large, new corporate transactions, if directly handled by the bank's treasury given the transactional size.

2.1.4 Unexpected cash flows

Transactions like large commercial financing, own bond issues or other capital funding are not treated as regular flows and will require case–by-case handling. They will have to be mapped on the cash flow ladder once terms and timelines are set. In addition to such transactions, as part of the management activity of planning and the bank's treasury it will be necessary to treat other flows that cannot be anticipated but may occur, such as rating downgrades. These will need gauging in the cash flow ladder as being part of the unexpected flows that need to be included.

2.1.5 Funds available for refinancing

Another element that should be included in the ladder is securities immediately available for repo or refinancing in the wholesale market. The securities and other marketable assets that are not yet pledged (referred to as 'unencumbered') at closing date should be included as a distinctive component and presented against the net result of cash flows.

We need to consider the haircut to assets and securities, reducing their value in the case of deteriorated market conditions: central bank (ECB, FED) haircuts or Basel 3 proposed haircuts must be considered in internal assessment and managerial valuation of the securities' marketability.

2.1.6 Funds transferability

In combining the flows of separate legal entities, the sum of the parts can be misleading as the legal transferability of funds across companies is not always permitted, at least fully. Greatest attention should be given to cross-border transferability, where limits both at company and regulatory level can severely hamper fund movements. Such analysis will be relevant for large banking groups with international legal entity presence: recent market crises have revealed that these are severe constraints that must be considered and valued before presenting consolidated evidence to management that could otherwise be misleading.

2.1.7 Total ladder calculation

We previously indicated a relevant factor to be considered in obtaining the cash flow ladder of diverse entities to get the group total cash flow ladder. In addition to actual funds transferability, other elements one needs to assess are currency conversions (the currency to use for group total versus the representation of each currency in the ladder separately), and the treatment of neither core currency nor domestic ones for the various legal entities that are part of a group. It is also important to present the assets available for refinancing as total available funds; but this too should be done to reflect the transferability assessment across entities and countries.

2.2 LIQUIDITY COVERAGE RATIO

We describe in this short-term funding chapter two main approaches to monitor and manage liquidity. The cash flow ladder, presented in the previous section, articulates the liquidity net flows in the coming days and months, supporting the bank treasury's timely and prompt intervention in the case that it is necessary to offset negative gaps. The liquidity cover ratio adds further elements such as the outflows in the next 30 calendar days. This way the LCR introduces an element of forecasting in the bank's prudential liquidity management. While the cash flow ladder is the actual gap position by maturity at the moment of calculation, the LCR is a limit given on cash flows versus available assets, adjusted by some prudential haircut or conservative factors that should take into account the asset's actual liquidity in the financial markets (see Chapter 3). The LCR is an important indicator of short-term liquidity exposure and allows management to consider the possible effects of deteriorating market conditions. For regulatory purposes, LCR should be recalculated on a daily basis, though for managerial purposes its calculation can be at less frequent intervals than the ladder, weekly rather than daily or intraday.

2.2.1 Regulatory prescriptions

Indications are given of the elements necessary to calculate the numerator and denominator of the LCR: the total stock of high quality liquid assets and the estimated outflows in 30 days:

$$LCR = \frac{\text{liquid assets available}}{\text{net cash outflows over 30 days}}$$

For regulatory purposes, banks should try to always maintain this ratio above 100%. It is plausible that the LCR will produce different results depending on the markets where the bank operates and depending on the balance sheet structure. This will be down to national supervisors setting further LCR sub-limits.

2.2.2 Liquid assets available for refinancing

The first requisite for assets to be included in the ratio is that they must not be pledged. It is necessary to know which securities are used for repo in the market. Highly liquid assets are the ones that *can be easily converted into cash at little or no loss of value*, the characteristics ensuring high liquidity being:

- Of large market in terms of volumes and participants' quotations (there are reliable market makers).
- Of contained credit and market risk (rating of the issuer and subordination) and correlation to other assets.
- Short maturity, contained volatility, inflation and currrency risks.
- Limited price uncertainty (in terms of valuation and price availability).

Liquid assets for secured funding are grouped into classes of varying credit quality. The most secure will likely keep their value and marketability. Weights for securities available for secured funding presented in the Basel 3 accord vary according to levels of decreasing quality: first-level assets being the highest in standard receive a weighting of 0%, second-level assets are assigned a 15%, 25% or 50% weighting, depending on the type of asset (regulators distinguish between Level 2A and Level 2B and list types and assigned haircuts). Some valuable statistic information is presented in Figure 2.2, taken from the European Banking Authority.

The stock of high-quality liquid assets should comprise assets with the characteristics outlined above. Here we describe the assets

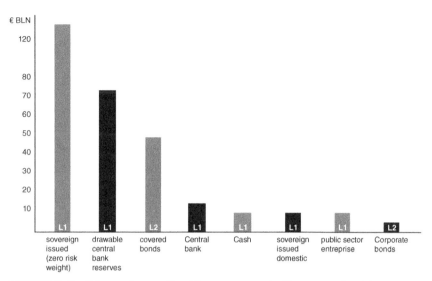

FIGURE 2.2 Most relevant liquid asset types in European banking, December 2012.
Source: EBA voluntary LCR monitoring exercise.

that are considered liquid and have the right characteristics to be included in the stock. For regulatory standards they are split into two classes or levels and can be included in the ratio's calculation: first-level assets can be included without limit, second-level assets can only count towards 40% of total stock.

The total amount of liquid assets is the impact on assets that would result if all short-term secured funding transactions, secured lending and collateral swap transactions were unwound. All high-quality liquid assets should ideally be central bank eligible for intra-day liquidity needs and overnight liquidity. In Figure 2.3 one finds each country's cumulative LCR.

First-level assets (also indicated as Level 1 assets) Most liquid assets can include an unlimited share of the pool, are held at market value and are subject to a 5% haircut for the LCR; the highest liquidity assets are just the ones listed below (see the Basel 3 accord for further details):

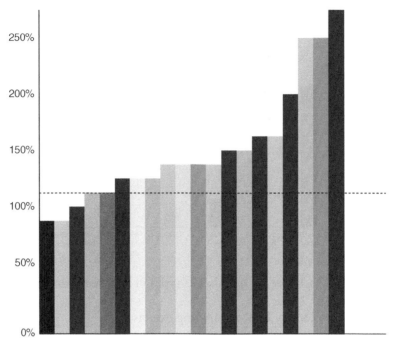

FIGURE 2.3 LCR by country: 2012 EBA exercise. EU aggregates – each column represents a country.

- Cash and central bank reserves that are not subject to prudential haircuts.
- Securities that are guaranteed by sovereigns (including central banks, public sector companies), the BIS, the IMF, the ECB and European Community, or multilateral development banks and that received a 0% risk weight based on the Basel II Standardized Approach for credit risk.
- In those circumstances when the sovereign has a non-0% risk weight, the domestic sovereign or central bank debt securities issued in foreign currencies are eligible up to the amount of the individual bank's stressed net cash outflows in that specific foreign currency (these being those in the jurisdiction where the liquidity is being withdrawn).

Second-level assets of highest quality (indicated as Level 2A)

These assets can be included in the stock as long as they do not surpass 40% of the overall stock, calculated once prudential haircuts have been applied. A minimum 15% haircut is applied to the market value of any second-level asset held in this Level 2A class, taking into account that these:

- Are marketable securities guaranteed by sovereigns, central banks or similar with a 20% risk weight under the Basel II Standardized Approach for credit risk (see above).
- Have a reliable record of liquidity source even during stressed market conditions (this is set as the maximum price drop below 10% or an increase in the prudential haircut under 10 percentage points over a 30-day period at times of liquidity stress).
- Are corporate debt securities (including commercial paper) and/or covered bonds. In the case of corporate debt securities, they should not be issued by a financial institution or its affiliated companies; for covered bonds, these too shall not be issued by the bank itself or its affiliated; securities are expected to have a AA-long-term credit rating of a recognized external credit assessment institution (ECAI) or a short-term rating equivalent in quality; alternatively, they can be rated by the bank with probability of default akin to a AA- rating. For these too there must be a record of transactions/liquidity during stressed market conditions, intended again as a maximum of 10% price drop or haircut raised over a 30-day period at times of significant liquidity stress.

Lower tier second-level assets (Level 2B)

In the new regulation, high-quality liquid assets can also include additional assets: these will be considered in the calculation of the resources available for liquidity funding and are indeed relevant for refinancing purposes. These additional assets are listed below:

- Securities guaranteed by residential mortgages[1] that received at least a AA credit rating.
- Securities issued by corporates rated from A+ to BBB-.
- Equity shares traded in the exchanges that are not issued by financial institutions (or affiliated companies).
- High-quality liquid assets that are pledged for a period of 6 months to one year.
- Interbank loans with banks under prudential supervision, also maturing in 6 months to one year.
- Interbank deposits that are kept for operational means.
- All other high-quality liquid assets maturing up to one year, including loans to non-financial, corporate clients, retail clients or small businesses, sovereigns and central banks.

The corporate debt securities will get a 50% haircut and will be included if they are not issued by a financial institution, have reliable market liquidity records, a long-term credit rating between A+ and BBB- from a ECAI or an equivalent short-term rating or an internal PD alike of between A+ and BBB-.

Equity shares will also get a 50% haircut and can be included if they are not issued by a financial firm, are exchange traded, centrally cleared, are part of the major stock index in the home jurisdiction, are traded in large and active markets, have a statistical liquidity record where, for maximum decline of market indexes price or increase in haircut, they stayed below 40% over a 30-day period.

The haircut applied then is 50%, much higher than those applicable to second-tier financial instruments but with higher ratings. The

---

[1]The underlying asset pool must be residential mortgages, cannot have structured products and must be of the kind that, in the event of foreclosure, the mortgage owner must remain liable, have a maximum loan-to-value ratio of 80% on average.

TABLE 2.2 Summary of levels and weights of the high-quality liquid assets.

Asset	Weight	Stock of high-quality liquid assets
Level 1	**100%**	Securities issued from sovereigns, central banks, public entities, develpment banks; coins & banknotes central bank reserves
		Domestic sovereign or central bank debt for non 0% risk-weighted sovereigns
Level 2A	**85%**	Assets with 20% risk weight isseued by sovereign, public entities, central banks, development banks
		Qualifying corporate debt securities rated AA- or higher
		Qualifying covered bonds rated AA- or higher
Level 2B	**75%**	Qualifying residential mortgage-backed securities
	50%	Qualifying corporate debt securities rated A+ to BBB-
	50%	Qualifying common equity shares

Source: The author and EBA.

total of a bank's assets held in the so-called Level 2B is subject to a maximum limit of 15%.

High-quality liquid assets that are eligible and the haircuts applied are summarized in Table 2.2.

2.2.3 Total net cash outflows in the upcoming month

The LCR's denominator is to be calculated as follows:

$$Total\ net\ outflows\ over\ the\ next\ 30\ calendar\ days =$$
$$total\ expected\ cash\ outflows - min\ (total\ expected\ cash\ inflows;$$
$$75\%\ total\ expected\ cash\ outflows)$$

Outflows and inflows must be calculated according to a set of rules, presented hereafter (see the summary tables). More details are

TABLE 2.3   Cash outflow types and weights applicable – first set.

Weight	Outflows
3%	Retail stable deposits with insurance scheme
5%	Retail stable deposits
10%	Retail less stable retail deposits
0%	Retail term deposits with residual maturity > 30 days
5%	Stable demand & term depos of small business with maturity < 30 days
10%	Less stable demand & term depos of SME with maturity < 30 days
25%	Operational depos generated by clearing, custody, cash mgmt,
5%	Operational depos generated by clearing, custody, cash mgmt with insurance coverage
25%	Cooperative banks in an institutional network
40%	Non financial corporates, sovereigns, development banks, public entities
20%	Non financial corporates, sovereigns, development banks, public entities with full coverage by deposit insurance
100%	Other legal entity customers
0%	Secured funding with central bank or backed by level 1 assets
15%	Secured funding backed by level 2A assets
25%	Secured funding with domestic sovereigns, development banks, public entities
25%	Secured funding backed by level 2B residential mortgage securities
50%	Secured funding backed by level 2B securities
100%	All other secured funding

Source: The author and EBA.

in the Basel Committee on Banking Supervision documentation for Liquidity Coverage Ratio of January 2013.

Outflows   The bank needs to determine, according to the set percentages presented in Tables 2.3 and 2.4, the financing outflows for the 30 days to come, and these will feed into the ratio calculation.

TABLE 2.4 Cash outflow types and weights applicable – second set, follows from previous table.

Weight	Outflows
3 notch down	Liquidity needs related to financing transactions, like collateral calls
20%	Valuation changes on non level 1 collateral posted on derivatives
100%	Excess collateral held by a bank related to derivative transactions that could contractually be called any time
100%	Liquidity needs related to collateral due from derivatives transactions
100%	Liabilities from maturing SIV, conduits, SPVs
100%	Asset-backed securities applied to maturing amounts
5%	Retail & SME undrawn committed credit & liquidity lines
10%	Undrawn committed credit lines to non financial corporates, sovereigns, central banks, development banks and public entities
30%	Undrawn committed liquidity lines to non financial corporates, sovereigns, central banks, development banks and public entities
40%	Undrawn committed credit & liquidity lines to banks subject to prudential supervision
30%	Undrawn committed credit lines to other financial institutions
100%	Undrawn committed liquidty lines to other financial institutions
100%	Undrawn committed credit & liquidty to all other legal entities
0–5%	Trade finance contingent funding liabilities
50%	Customer short positions covered by other customers' collateral

Source: The author and EBA.

Unlike earlier consultative papers, the indications from the Basel Committee on Banking Supervision are indeed detailed and also prescriptive on behavioural elements such as deposit stability. As we can see, the stickiness weights are assigned according to clear, detailed rules, ensuring a level playing field: only a very few parameters will be left to individual banks' and local regulator's determination and then full disclosure shall be provided. In assessing and classifying deposit stability, an important element will be describing and analysing the government insurance programme in force, verifying that it has the ability to ensure prompt payouts for which the coverage is clearly defined and awareness is high amongst depositors (here an awareness campaign or questionnaire could prove useful). In particular, the rules set to identify which retail deposits are to be considered stable and then get a 3% weight prescribe that these ought to have a state insurance scheme covering them in full; in addition, the insurance scheme to allow a 3% outflow rate (rather than a higher 5%) must be based on a regular and specific government levy on banks and rely on adequate cash and reserve stock in case of large withdrawal by depositors, with clear legal terms and in the absence of long-term notices.

As we can see, there is a 10% or higher outflow rate for less stable retail deposits, these being the ones that do not fall within the fully covered types (3% or 5% rates) and are either private banking or wealthier individuals that as such might be expected to be more volatile and more likely to react faster in the case of a liquidity crisis. This also applies to retail deposits that we cannot clearly assign to the lower outflow rate categories.

Regarding term deposits, if there is no legal right to withdraw within the 30 days or this results in a loss greater than the due interest, then we can exclude it from outflows. If, instead, we let customers withdraw cash and do not apply the penalty for commercial or reputational reasons, then these shall be considered demand deposits.

The case for deposits of small corporates or local business customers is slightly different and experience shows here that their behaviour is akin to that of the private customers. Supervisors are indeed assuming so with outflow minimum thresholds for stable and less stable customer deposits. The definition of a small business in Basel is one with deposits below one million Euros.

For derivatives, including interest swaps that are the largest part of banks' treasury OTC activity, contractually set amounts payable and receivable must be considered in the flows and these should also be net of specific collateral posting, making sure the collateral is not counted twice in the counterbalancing capacity stock (we must be sure the securities available for refinancing are not pledged).

An important risk factor to consider is the additional/unexpected liquidity needs in the case of a downgrade of the institution's ratings by an agency: here the effect varies depending on the derivatives or other transactions in place and the contractual terms. Impacts vary substantially depending on the severity of the downgrade and confirmation of downgrades by several agencies. Financial transactions of the bank with other institutions typically require additional collateral (usually highly rated securities, so affecting the available stock for refinancing) or cash or even repayment/partial termination in case of downgrades. Though these can be anticipated to a certain extent as agencies pay regular visits and their assessment is an ongoing process, downgrade additional collateral posting can barely be forecast and managed more than six months in advance: this leaves some time to arrange the posting or find the necessary corrective actions, but might prove complex in rapidly deteriorating market conditions as these result in a domino-like effect, so exponentially penalizing weaker banks.

Another important factor we must assess is the credit lines contractually assured to clients, those that are contractually binding and irrevocable obligations to provide liquidity to retail or corporate customers. These are typically off-balance-sheet facilities, often provided as part of the commercial relationship with customers and regularly rolled over. In stressed market conditions, such facilities must be closely monitored as lines still available could be withdrawn by clients in difficulty. Likewise, contractual loans with contractual binding facilities expected to be granted should be fully included in the outflows forecasts.

There are then also some contingent funding obligations that may be contractual or non-contractual and are different from credit arrangements. Amongst these are instruments like unconditionally revocable uncommitted credit and liquidity facilities or guarantees and letters of credit; potential requests for debt repurchases of the bank's own debt or that of related conduits; structured products like adjustable/variable rate notes; managed funds like money market mutual funds or other collective investment funds distributed to own clients. For banks ensuring securities' market-making bid and offer prices, there may be a need to include a number of securities to cover the potential repurchase of outstanding securities.

Inflows Similar analysis as that performed to estimate the outflows must be carried out to forecast inflows. The Basel Committee, in setting the inflows rate, set limits to inflows trying to assure a prudential balance with the total expected cash outflows, this is to force additional prudential requirements and a larger amount held of liquid assets (supervisors apply a prudential logic based on contractual obligation and assume full or large outflows or limited inflows in the cases of no explicit binding obligations). Though understandable from a prudential standpoint, more customer statistical-based analysis and knowledge in order to gauge the flow prediction in different market conditions would probably provide a better estimate (likewise for the capital at risk calculation, allowing for internal models would have been a preferable approach). As anticipated, for supervisors the bank should only include contractual inflows from credit which are fully performing and where there is no evidence that a default may occur in the short term (and surely in the coming 30-day horizon). As part of inflow liquidity management, an important control is the concentration of clients, both in terms of size and number, ensuring an unexpected difficulty with a large customer may pose

TABLE 2.5 Cash inflow types and weights applicable.

Weight	Inflows
0%	Maturing secured lending backed by level 1 asset
15%	Maturing secured lending backed by level 2A asset
25%	Maturing secured lending backed by level 2B eligible RMBS
50%	Maturing secured lending backed by level 2B other assets
50%	Margin lending backed by all other collateral
100%	All other assets
0%	Credit & liquidity facilities provided to the reporting bank
0%	Operational deposits held at other financial institutions
50%	Amounts from retail counterparties
50%	Amounts from non financial wholesale counterparties
100%	Amounts from financial institutions and central banks
100%	Net derivatives cash inflows

Source: The author and EBA.

a severe problem to the institution refinancing. The weights applied are presented in Table 2.5.

Supervisors assume that banks will not be hampered from using credit lines or liquidity facilities granted to them by other banks. Here it might be difficult to ascertain in practice the management and utilization of these facilities: as the lines will be typically unsecured and uncommitted, the market conditions will vary and might have a gradual impact on interbank relations such as to render such a prudential stance partially unrealistic at some stages of crisis.

For all other types of transactions, either secured or unsecured, the inflow rate will be determined by counterparty type. Regulators are assuming that the bank will get all performing contractual inflows from retail and small business customers, this being the case unless a bank experiences a repeated deterioration of customer repayment capacity. Whether this is a proper prudential approach remains to be seen, as small businesses proved the most affected in countries like Italy, Spain and Portugal during the recent crisis and performing loans rapidly deteriorated in many banks' credit portfolios. At the same time, however, regulators for the liquidity requirements calculation want banks to continue to provide loans to retail and small business customers.

For derivatives contracts in place, inflows can be assumed in full, and amounts payable and receivable should be accounted on a net basis, as indicated for the outflows before.

An important variable to control, especially for international banks, is the different currency in which it operates and the specific liquidity: we discussed this in presenting the cash flow ladder analysis and it also impacts the ratio calculation. Regulators require the ratio to be reported in a single common currency, banks must meet their liquidity needs in each currency and maintain high-quality liquid assets in line with these needs by currency: the treasury should clearly monitor liquidity exposure by currency and set aside separate securities stock for each, ideally issued in the same currency, as the bank might be expected to use the stock to gain liquidity in the currency and country where the cash outflows occur. The ratio is then to be calculated by the individual relevant currency and each should be monitored and reported to the treasury and control functions. The bank will identify currency mismatches in this way and intervene if necessary: being exposed to foreign exchange liquidity requirements, we ought to remember that there is a concrete risk that the possibility of swapping currencies or accessing the relevant foreign exchange markets may deteriorate under stressed conditions and the exchange rate movements could affect our liquidity exposure. This is particularly relevant for less liquid or minor currencies.

2.3 LIQUIDITY RISK INDICATORS

Useful information and signals for managing risk can also be found in specific market indicators. As per other risk types, it is common practice to monitor several market data indexes that will help in forecasting or anticipating changes in risk levels. There is no definitive literature on the funding liquidity topic, a generic approach is presented in the Basel 3 document, thus it will be left to the individual organization and risk manager to identify meaningful liquidity risk indicators. Of foremost importance is making clear that the liquidity risk indicators are neither a standard list of separate specific indexes nor a minimum regulatory requirement; the stance is to add additional monitoring and assess whether it is adding any further value and information to the other reporting and measures calculated (LCR, NSFR, VaR, etc.).

We deem some market information useful for monitoring, primarily we would recommend a regular check, amongst others, on macroeconomic data releases and trends (such as production levels, unemployment, inflation, house sales, consumer confidence), commodities' levels (crude oil and grain prices, gold and base metals, gas), main foreign currency levels, government bond curves, spreads, credit default swaps for sovereigns and banks and central bank refinancing statistics. This is surely merely an indicative list and will need careful assessment and internal review for risk managers to select the most appropriate information; we will now address some elements we believe to be useful for the valuation of relevant market data.

2.3.1 Using indicators

Needless to say, indicators of many sorts are widely used in companies. As per banks, indicators for risk monitoring are widespread. Identifying which indicators are best to monitor liquidity risk is often a matter of selecting from a vast number of reports and market data produced and distributed internally every day from many functions' front to back offices. So the very first thing to have in mind when approaching liquidity risk indicators is that it is more a matter of selecting from existing sets than searching for new, specific types (for these we propose some at the end of the chapter). Once we have identified a range of meaningful liquidity indicators, we consider some critical issues:

- The possibility of getting these (feeding) daily and/or intraday.
- Applicability and/or articulation into subsets for business lines and countries.
- Benchmarking to competitors.

It is important that the data feeding is easy and does not require complex technology infrastructure and investment, and ideally information should be retrieved from market sources during the day too. Likewise, it is also relevant to consider (i) whether indicators are available for many markets and countries, and (ii) if it is possible to articulate these into sets applicable to individual business lines (indicators could prove useful in spreading and allocating liquidity charges internally and to customers). Lastly, (iii) the comparison of results is often a plus or a necessity, as understanding where one stands versus the industry is particularly important in driving strategy and management decisions (it is also useful in regulatory and rating agency discussions).

2.3.2 Testing indicators

Standard statistical techniques are good for assessing an indicator's predictive power in terms of liquidity risks, I will not list them here or go into detail on those one should prefer, as they are available in many specific time series analysis papers and texts and standard statistics books. Here we shall look at the decision process one should apply and follow in the selection process. First, one should aim to split the indicators into predictive ones – the kind that can anticipate possible future dynamics and are then capable of predicting to a certain extent a financial crisis (assuming these repeat themselves in similar forms) – and those of a more risk-monitoring type – measuring the changes in risk levels.

2.3.3 Government bond yield curves and cross-spreads

The shape of the government curve is a revealing indicator of liquidity market conditions. Analysing dynamics of the yield curve shape, the way the shape changes before and during a crisis, can help in forecasting the development of liquidity markets. In particular, one should follow the historical changes of major markets before and following each crisis and see how the yield curve for government bonds both prices liquidity and sovereign risk. If we look at government curve behaviours then we see the changes at first glance. The things we notice and are held in common are the change in volatility, the shape of the curves (curve shape structural changes, e.g. steepening/flattening), the sudden modification of historical ranges in correlation and spreads between maturities, countries and currencies. In short, the crisis is reflected in these rate changes, both in the months beforehand and during. As the exact time of beginning and ending might be uncertain, one should look at time frames and structural breaks that are easier to identify.

2.3.4 Credit default swap levels

As markets reflect risk assessment, CDS spreads on government curves are important for monitoring possible deterioration of credit worth. Both the absolute value and the volatility of CDS spreads on government curves are interesting indicators and should be monitored. CDS are not always a definitive valuation of actual risk as they also depend on market volumes; for most liquid markets and G7 countries these are indeed a good track of risk premium levels.

It might be useful to look at CDS levels on individual banking stocks, mostly large international banking groups, as the liquidity risk is transmitted through the wholesale financial markets.

2.3.5 Foreign exchange cross-values

The relative strength or weakness of an individual currency indicates market sentiment. Past liquidity crises show common elements and trends, for example commodity prices or cross-currency rates, market indexes and economic confidence levels. Likewise, as liquidity is a concern for payment capacity, cross-currency rates will reflect countries' refinancing capacity as perceived by the markets. There has often been a redirection of funds away from riskier countries and their currencies towards safer, or so perceived, ones. Possibly, clustering countries' currencies, for example the G7 and G20 ones, and monitoring the cross-rate volatility within the groups and across groups, might be useful.

2.3.6 Central bank refinancing

Refinancing rates and deposits held at central banks are key to predicting liquidity shortages. As trust in wholesale markets wanes, evidence shows lending to market counterparties reduces or halts and deposits at the central bank peak. In addition, monitoring it is valuable to monitor the bank's overall monetary aggregates, and in particular its short-term deposits and overnight deposits position. It is useful to look at the variation of M3 counterparties' central banks money market rates.

2.3.7 Crisis indicators

Some indicators – or indexes – have been developed and regularly published that can prove useful for anticipating a financial crisis, then a liquidity stress condition. We would like to look more closely at some, presented hereafter, this being an indicative list rather than an exhaustive one – which would require a dedicated work in itself (see bibliography) – and presented as an additional type of variable one could be looking at in forecasting liquidity risk.

1. Arouba Diebold Scotti Business Conditions Index (ADS BCI in the Bloomberg). This is maintained by the Federal Reserve Bank of Philadelphia, and it is designed to monitor business conditions at regular and close intervals. It relies on a mix of

major economic indicators (e.g. the US weekly initial jobless claims; monthly payroll employment, industrial production, personal income less transfer payments, manufacturing and trade sales; and quarterly real GDP; we must be aware that these statistics are frequently revised and updated at different times, so affecting the index). It allows one, on its update, to have a feeling of the overall level of US economic activity, therefore it is indeed indirectly providing a liquidity risk signal when it deteriorates. Importantly, it is available in real time from standard data providers (e.g. Bloomberg). It is modelled to get an average value of zero: if we got a value of −0.7 then this would be an alarm signal and it might be interpreted as an increased liquidity risk or a risk of a liquidity crisis occurring.

2. The Eurocoin Growth Indicator, New Eurocoin. This index focuses on the Eurozone economic activity and it is commonly quoted as one of the major indicators of European business conditions. This is also an indicator available real time from common data providers. It is a monthly updated forecast of Euro area GDP growth: it is constructed to take into account seasonality elements and it is soon available once official data are published. These first two indicators, including the Arouba Diebold Scotti, focus on the economy conditions (GDP, unemployment, manufacturing levels): there are other ones that can also be used and might be better suited, the important element to consider is whether data are timely and frequently updated and parameters applied (e.g. weights) are also disclosed.

3. Germany ZEW indicator of economic sentiment. For this very important indicator, a survey is carried out of 350 financial experts and it is meant to show the difference between those that are optimistic and those that instead feel pessimistic for the economic condition in six months' time. Though it is country specific, it is highly regarded and it has a major impact on market sentiment given the importance of Germany within the Euro zone.

4. US Economic Policy Uncertainty indicator. This is based on the concept that political instability is negative for prices and that political volatility reflects badly on economic conditions. The uncertainty indicator is based on three different sets of parameters: first we have the monthly news articles containing the words 'uncertain' or 'uncertainty', 'economic' or 'economy', and policy-relevant terms; these are then scaled by the number of articles containing 'today'. We then combine the number of tax laws expiring in coming years and lastly we include a mix of quarterly updates on government expenditure and the one-year consumer price index (here it is the Philadelphia Fed Survey of Forecasters). This index differs from the economic data-based indexes or economic sentiment measures and adds a further parameter to our forecasting tool: the qualitative assessment of political development, this being a major element that could trigger high market volatility (an example is the rapid and extreme swings linked to quantitative easing by the European Central Banks, and how this is impacting asset valuations – and in turn banks' counterbalancing capacity).

5. Citigroup Surprise index is a measure of whether typically the economic reports have been better or worse than the economists' consensus. This is another kind of qualitative and forward-looking indicator on macroeconomic changes. Like the ZEW, this is a benchmark of data results versus expectations of surveyed financial analysts and economists. Whether this fares better than other, similar types of indicators is of lesser importance: we should indeed select a few of these indicators and combine them to more standard, financial market data (index levels, inflation and rates) and start monitoring them in a combined fashion. Through time, the set should evolve, adding or replacing indicators or parameters, changing the frequency of some and possibly combining each with weights and correlations. The real test will be future events, from there we shall take empirical indications and modify our forecasting indicators tool set.

2.3.8 Risk aversion indexes

Many have computed and proposed indices to measure risk aversion. Fluctuations in investor risk aversion are often cited as a factor explaining crises on financial markets. The alternation between periods of bullishness prompting investors to make risky investments, and periods of bearishness when they retreat to the safest forms of investments, could be at the root of sharp fluctuations in asset prices. One problem in the assessment of these different periods is in clearly distinguishing the risk perceived by agents from risk aversion itself. Some analyses use raw series to estimate changes in investors' perception of risk. For instance, the price of gold may be used if we assume that, during periods of uncertainty, investors will reallocate their wealth to assets traditionally perceived as safe, such as gold. The same would be true of the Swiss franc exchange rate.

The implied volatility of options is also used. For example, the volatility index (VIX) created by the Chicago Board Options Exchange in 1993 is the implied volatility on the S&P 500. It is regarded by many market analysts as a direct gauge of fear. Several indicators have been created by aggregating elementary series. These measures are relatively simple to put in place and can be easily interpreted. In most cases, they are weighted averages of a number of variables. Indicators of this type are JP Morgan's liquidity, credit and volatility index, the UBS risk index, Merrill Lynch's financial stress index and the risk perception indicator of the Caisse des Dépôts et Consignations.

Theoretically, an increase in risk aversion should lead to an increase in risk premia across all markets, but the increase should be greater on the riskiest markets. This is the idea on which the global risk aversion index (GRAI) is based, devised by Persaud (1996). Changes in risk aversion are represented by the correlation between price variations of different securities and their volatility: if the correlation is positive, risk aversion has decreased; if the correlation is negative, it has increased. In practice, if we wish the GRAI to increase with risk aversion, the correlation must be given a negative sign. Instead of a correlation, a regression coefficient between price variations and volatilities may also be used (which is also given a negative sign). The indicator is then called the risk aversion index (RAI). From a theoretical standpoint, the construction is based on simplifying assumptions that are probably not borne out in reality; notably, the independence of excess returns and the independence between expected future prices and variations in risk aversion. Another limitation of this indicator is that it does not measure levels of risk aversion but rather changes in it. The correlation coefficient only makes it possible to distinguish periods in which risk aversion has increased from those in which it has fallen.

From an empirical point of view, the GRAI and RAI also display some limitations. First, the measurements show that these indicators are extremely volatile. This seems counter-intuitive, as a good indicator should be stable during quiet periods. Second, changes in the indicator over time differ quite markedly depending on the period chosen for the calculations of volatility of returns as well as on the market concerned.

2.4 INTRADAY LIQUIDITY RISK

So far we have discussed liquidity requirements in terms of end of day nets and projected cash flows for the coming days and weeks. Probably as important is the intraday management and that collateral posting and assurance payments are met in a timely manner is also fundamental and must be controlled. The assumptions that the next day requirements are captured in the liquidity net cash flow projections still cannot anticipate intraday volatility and volumes. The possibility of an exceptional event in particular needs evaluating, as these can occur suddenly and force exceptional collateral posting or drained market funding.

When managing intraday liquidity, we must rely on cash and collateral management systems that take into account the wholesale payment and settlement systems to ensure actual intraday monitoring, as the payments funnel through these.

2.4.1 Intraday liquidity management

Liquidity sources for intraday financing are reserve balances at the central bank or eligible collateral not pledged with another bank that can be freely transferred to the central bank and converted into central bank money; committed or uncommitted credit lines available intraday and balances with other banks that can be used for settlement on the same day.

The size, nature and speed of payment regulations are such that banks – and especially large international ones – have huge regulation flows in terms of nominal value and numbers of transactions during the day. Over the last few decades, changes in payment and settlement systems have followed these needs and increased intraday liquidity requirements, increasing intraday monitoring/control awareness. For international banks and most active financial institutions, this implies foreign exchange operations, different time zones, real-time settlements and flow patter through the day.

Intraday management of cash flows must ensure the balance of cash in and out and collateral valuation control to meet operational needs: clearly, considering the amounts and the frequency that a bank's treasury needs to manage, this requires adequate and reliable technology systems; accurate day net flows planning, addressing peaks and seasonality; matching information from payments and settlement networks; simulation of different stress/scenario based anomalies on these; and dedicated control functions and dispute management processes.

Intraday liquidity management of flow payments hinges on a sound process involving front and back office functions. As it is structured for close monitoring of the expected payments and involves direct contacts with counterparties – especially for misalignments and possible disputes – the mechanism in place should ensure a rapid and effective management of problems hampering payments and settlements. We can be managing the settlement systems by applying either net or gross netting, however of the utmost importance for liquidity risk is that intraday payment obligations are met and match the expected flows. We should therefore have a back office process and monitoring mechanism in place allowing for immediate intervention in case problems emerge during the day, and also have a set of alert indicators that allow forward-looking and preventive intervention. Going back to the section on liquidity risks, the statistics on intraday payments will prove extremely useful and are therefore worth analysing: we might be looking for averages, volumes and volatility by groups and individual counterparties, type of transactions, collateral posted and liquidity line intraday utilization. These are particularly useful combined with market information and credit indications on counterparties provided by internal credit departments, analysing the overall exposure and a breakdown on issuer, short-term, long-term, pre-settlement and settlement risks.

We are required by regulators – and indeed this is a sound management practice – to include intraday liquidity management in the overall liquidity risk control processes. We should have it as part of the risk management framework, with specific internal procedures and policies for intraday liquidity that ought to be presented and approved by the bank's relevant functions and bodies, including the Board of Directors. The intraday liquidity management processes should then encompass the following:

- The monitoring and control of intraday liquidity positions, forecasting intraday timing of payment and inflows.
- An adequate intraday source of funding to meet the intraday needs.
- Emergency or contingency procedures to tackle unexpected operational problems in the payment systems.

We are typically managing intraday payment flows so that they end the day matched and the value of incoming payments is aligned to the outflows: the bank's treasury function manages the liquidity of intraday exposures, ensuring these are closed within the working day. Intraday exposures can be very significant in nominal and risk amounts and banks can often have significant intraday liquidity exposures even to individual counterparties; this would usually be towards other banks and such intraday risk exposures can reach very significant levels such that bilateral liquidity needs might be huge, requiring relevant collateral posting.

Another factor we need to closely monitor is the intraday facilities provided by the settlement banks to the active members: the latter can be leveraged on the settlement bank to ensure liquidity needs, once again generating potentially significant liquidity exposures. This is particularly the case for banks providing settlement services, thereby exposing them and therefore the payment systems as a whole to the largest intraday liquidity risk. Thus we should also include the intraday payments in the stress testing and scenario analysis and have an assessment of the potential impact of hampered credit facilities from our settlement banks: this must be part of the regular stress testing and scenario analysis and be the base for sound contingency planning (see Chapter 5 for more on liquidity contingency funding plans).

One can even anticipate from anomalies in the payment or the settlement systems whether a financial crisis risk or some abnormal market condition could be occurring. The monitoring of intraday liquidity was a key indicator and survival factor during stressed market conditions, so there was a strong argument supporting holding additional security buffers for intraday unexpected claims. As the cost of intraday liquidity was very low, such practices led to situations where settlement banks provided liquidity to the entire system and allowed payments to be settled throughout the day smoothly and without delays (see Table 2.6 for the trend on transactions processed through central payment systems). Banks are now required to

TABLE 2.6 Payments processed by selected interbank fund transfer systems.

		2006	2007	2008	2009	2010
Payment system	a) total transactions sent in millions					
	b) value transaction €bln					
TARGET	a)	83	99	89	88	87
	b)	539	675	611	538	634
EURO1/STEP1	a)	48	54	64	58	59
	b)	48	58	73	65	62
STEP2 XCT	a)	66	91	73	54	46
	b)	267	361	315	224	204
STEP2 ICT	a)	-	221	265	287	301
	b)	-	995	1305	1193	1226

Source: European Central Bank.

calculate their intraday liquidity needs and just to hold a proportion of the requisite assets. Sound liquidity risk management will see security buffers gradually increased to cover intraday liquidity risk too, this will affect the cost of intraday liquidity and the willingness of banks to ensure liquidity.

Banks are nowadays settling payments on a gross basis and it is necessary to have sufficient funds in their settlement accounts immediately available for these payments. Banks can rely on liquidity coming from inflows to match dues and this proves useful during the day as timing differences can result in problematic payment issues: here the back office or the bank's treasury should look at the schedule of flows during the day and plan both the funds buffer in their settlement account and also the optimal timing to ensure due cash outflows and inflows match, as the absolute overall value of the intraday flows typically outsizes the net at the end of the day. Settlement banks meet intraday liquidity needs using their own funds and reserves but can rely on repo using available collateral or directly through the money markets. It is important to know that for most payment systems the settlement does not need to be carried out at a specific time during the day, so leaving some intraday flexibility to banks to ensure payments, so that we can get additional liquidity if necessary (exceptions to this flexibility are, for example, CLS for the global foreign exchange markets and the central counterparty clearing, CCP, as one can see in Figure 2.4).

For settlement banks, it is possible to forecast large payment flows so their matching flow management is much easier than for participating banks and can predict liquidity requirements – benefiting from their pivotal role in payments especially when it comes to the largest transactions. The settlement banks can also apply statistical techniques similar to those used to predict sight deposit behaviour to payment flows, so also simplifying the process, reducing costs and optimizing liquidity stock requirements. In cases of market stress conditions, the settlement banks might reduce or even be forced to halt transaction handling: here, too, the possible use of indicators to anticipate problems or anomalies at market or counterparty level can prove extremely valid. On the other hand, banks participating need to have detailed operational procedures to reduce the risk of error occurring and also to have appropriate back-up mechanisms if problems occur.

2.4.2 Cooperative mechanism

Intraday payment systems function by relying on a mutual trust mechanism where participants can use the inflows of payment made by one bank to fund, in turn, their payments during the day for free; this being the convenience of building a cooperative exchange. Such a mechanism works as long as there is a mutual benefit and fair, cooperative behaviour of the members: if one participant instead stops or delays payments due, while still receiving those the other banks are obliged to give, it will affect the system as a whole, kindling a chain reaction that might affect all the banks in the system, as gradually all will experience delayed payments and thus reduce the possibility of

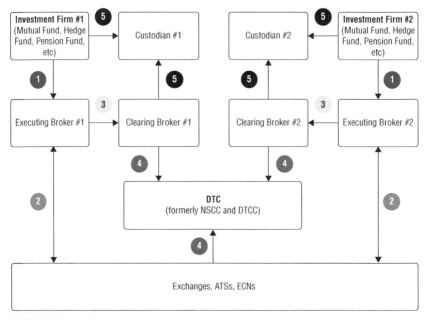

FIGURE 2.4 **1** These orders are routed from the Investment Firms (one is a buyer, the other is a seller) to their respective Executing Brokers.
2 The Executing Brokers send the orders to the appropriate Marketplace for the security being traded. The Marketplaces respond with executions ('fills').
3 The Executing Brokers send the fills to the Clearing Broker that was designated by the Investment Firms. Many Executing Brokers are themselves Clearing Brokers, a process which is called 'self-clearing'.
4 The Marketplace(s) and the Clearing Brokers compare their shares/money to make sure that they match. This is referred to as 'Street-Side matching'.
5 The Investment Managers inform their respective Custodians what they should expect to receive/deliver from the Clearing Brokers, and the Custodians perform this comparison. This is referred to as 'Customer-Side matching'. This occurs the day of the trade (T+0). On the Settlement Date (which is usually up to 3 days after the Trade Date, the date when the actual trade occurred), the Clearing Brokers will deliver/receive the match amount of shares/money to settle the trade with both Investment Firms.
Source: Wikipedia. Flowchart explanatory notes.

matching intraday payments as scheduled and according to a typical refunding liquidity mechanism. It is a delicate equilibrium, based on trust, which, if breached, could trigger a chain reaction.

The participants tend to avoid delayed payments because there will be fines and reputational impacts, as well as the risk of liquidity chain reactions as described before. Systems or settlement banks charge a fee for the use of intraday liquidity, varying from case to case (size and length of time, country, exchange); in some cases, intraday liquidity can be free of charge but requires eligible collateral posting. Here banks should consider, both in funding liquidity management and in their strategy for counterbalancing capacity securities stock, the potential buffers for the intraday liquidity requirements too. It must be said that in normal market conditions, securities clearing and smooth intraday flow replenishment during the day ensure the intraday liquidity cost for banks remains very low: in short, for the system to work, banks ensure timely payments during the day, limiting functioning risk to the system as a whole but also to the settlement banks.

2.4.3 Analysing the possible impact of the stressed scenario on intraday liquidity risk

Payment systems are exposed to conditions and events producing delays in intraday matching payments between participants, as this forces an increase in the stock of intraday securities to ensure timely payments. There are different stress situations that the bank should assess related to intraday funding liquidity:

- Difficulties on the side of the bank itself, where some events like the bank being downgraded or reputational impacts could hamper its capacity to get credit or financing.
- An operational problem or other type suffered by one of the major counterparties in the payment system, so leading to problems and delays in the entire system.

- Significant deterioration in assets posted as collateral, reducing the capacity of many participants to ensure smooth payment settlement.
- Technological or electrical outages of some sort, including program errors, as experienced in some exceptional cases, could also trigger exchange-wide problems.

As described above, banks rely on intraday payments from counterparties to ensure cash outflows, contractual obligations combined with statistical intraday timelines applied to manage intraday cash stocks and collateral posting. This mutual or chained behaviour mechanism allows intraday liquidity payments matching and reduces significantly the actual need of banks to inject cash and securities: it works as a natural netting scheme, substantially lowering the gross value of payments in the end. If a bank is mostly reliant on netting and incoming payments, though, then it may also be very exposed if there are liquidity market stress events or any situation that hampers the cooperative trust mechanism. Particularly alarming are reputational events that could affect one of the participant banks as this can lead to the other member banks reducing or stopping intraday payments towards the one affected: when such a situation occurs, the bank hit by such a reputational exposure will be suffering from other counterparty banks, questioning its capacity to meet payments. In such a situation, other banks' credit officers might demand that they receive payments before they make any, so interrupting the vital mutual intraday exchange mechanism. The effects for the bank are delayed or reduced cash inflows and intraday mismatch of expected in and out cash flows.

Such an event, striking first one of the payment system members, could generate a credit crunch where the settlement bank does not get liquidity as expected and even stops ensuring payments to the participating counterparty in difficulty. The troubled member, in turn, will have to use more of its own funds to ensure payments. In these situations the correspondent banks provide intraday credit to clients and payments are met using the settlement bank resources: in these cases, the settlement bank will be the one then exposed, adding then the many counterparties it could be providing such facilities to, it might end up bearing a system of credit exposure. The chain effect is then triggered and if one of the largest banks participating in a cooperative mechanism delays or halts payments, it might hamper the mutual trust-based process, subsequently hampering system payments and triggering a domino effect: the settlement banks could end up having to guarantee intraday payments and in the extreme situation if they stopped providing payments to individual troubled banks, it could trigger a rapid decline in the possibility of them meeting payments. In turn, this will have a multiplier effect on payment capacity.

2.4.4 Haircuts to pledges

We also need to monitor and manage intraday liquidity needs in the securities portfolio immediately available for refinancing, assessing the possible impact of stress testing and scenario indications on payment requirements. As described, when systemic problems occur, the market value of securities used for collateral posting or refinancing could diminish significantly in some cases. This could widen the bid-ask spreads and may impact the banks' capacity to sell large individual positions (see Chapter 4). This then will generate a higher haircut to securities or require the bank to set aside greater stock requirements as the market value diminishes. There could also be a situation where some asset may no longer be eligible for central bank refinancing facilities, if specific credit rating criteria are affected. Difficult market conditions, deteriorated reputational perceptions of some banks or any delayed payments could lead financial counterparties to demand additional collateral posting to ensure payments. Typically, settlement banks use sophisticated models to optimize intraday payment flows smoothly, as well as diminishing the impact of intraday liquidity stress. Such models may automatically stop payments to some counterparties, as they are set up and linked to specific limits on funds ensured, considering intraday liquidity facilities utilization: we must remember that such intraday liquidity and credit lines are often uncommitted.

2.4.5 Monitoring requirements

Supervisors are aware of the relevance of intraday liquidity risk and require financial institutions to closely control such exposure, in combination with the overall liquidity needs of the bank, ensuring there is the capacity to measure expected inflows and outflows as well as forecasting the intraday timing and the range of potential net funding for additional unexpected needs that might arise during the day. The importance of monitoring intraday liquidity for the scheduled payments, measuring in a timely manner the available resources and managing the available liquidity of unpledged financial resources available accordingly is also stressed, so we are relying on sufficient intraday funding to meet the intraday payments. Another important factor to manage and plan carefully is the possibility of managing and having immediate collateral available to obtain intraday funds. We are also asked to set up intraday liquidity limits and reporting for the various payment flows. We must also carry out regular stress and scenario analysis, filing payment statistical data for such a purpose.

2.4.6 Structural and intraday liquidity needs

If a bank is in funding liquidity difficulties or has structural problems that could even lead to deposits being withdrawn, this will end up affecting its intraday payments and available securities for refinancing too. Such an unfortunate case (such as the Northern Rock bank case) should be seen as rare and extreme. In such an event the central bank will have to step in to reassure markets and depositor trust. Central banks may use available assets to meet the payment need and reassure depositors, banks and market participants. This can further increase problems in ensuring payments both at interbank and to depositors, as happened to Lehman Brothers when its correspondent banks demanded increasing collateral posting for their intraday needs and these assets were taken from the bank's counterbalancing stock and thus couldn't be used to pay creditors. In normal conditions the probability of this happening is low, as banks keep a large enough stock of unpledged securities, far larger than intraday liquidity needs. One ought to build in normal market conditions security stocks to withstand longlasting liquidity stress too. We should be encouraged, therefore, to include as a separate item in the estimation of counterbalancing capacity stock the portion that it is meant for the liquidity funding of intraday needs, including the stress condition estimates. When using all of the securities available, particularly in times of stress, the bank's responsible function must be to carefully keep track of the two components: the structural stock to offset balance sheet deposits and payment requirements, from the intraday. The latter are surely a component of the overall balance sheet ladder but as they have the immediate result of exposing the bank to actual payment default the next day, we believe they are best managed as conceptually separate. Evidence that the intraday separated buffer is regularly fully used might be a strong indication that this needs rebalancing, thus increasing the preference for separate monitoring and management of this portion of available securities and cash. This should also appear in the intraday liquidity risk internal framework, and so in the internal policy, limit setting and reporting.

An intraday liquidity buffer should ensure that there are sufficient intraday funds to match due payments and that liquidity shocks do not hamper this capacity; so, as indicated before, it should be considered a key risk driver to determine a bank's asset buffer structural requirements. A distinct intraday liquidity buffer will permit the best handling of market stress conditions. Payment systems data are the starting point to calibrate intraday specific buffers. Some may argue that ring-fencing the assets held for the specific requirements of intraday payments is inefficient and will just lead to higher stock of highly rated but low-yielding securities, affecting banks' profitability without an actual practical benefit at times of crisis as banks can always rely on unencumbered stock to ensure refinancing also for the intraday. If applied as a regulatory rule, it could also hamper prompt payments in the cooperative system as banks will be increasingly trying to minimize this burden's impact. As it stands, there is a trade-off between risk aversion, prudential regulation and sustainability. The point here is to make sure in times of stress and market difficulties that there are the resources to ensure stability, payments and regular business.

2.4.7 Payment systems' liquidity saving features

Liquidity optimization mechanisms hinge on common features, one being an offsetting model that finds groups of payments that can be settled at the same time, greatly reducing liquidity requirements. Another useful element is a liquidity reservation mechanism indicating to the bank when to build liquidity stock for specific intraday large payments in order to settle these promptly, and at the same time to maintain a larger portion of liquidity available so that we are given a liquidity optimization process where one knows sufficiently far ahead when we need to ensure large payments, when this will occur and to what extent it overlaps with other relevant payments. Well-managed payment system participants handle cash flows according to priority and their urgent payments are processed first, while less relevant ones are settled through a queue-like mechanism, typically managed using a model that processes the payments due and offsets those to be settled at the same time. Penalties for delayed payments or collateral posting could help prompt settlement, and schemes of increasing costs for delayed payments, possibly weighted by size, are also designed to encourage such behaviour in the participants.

2.4.8 Intraday liquidity risk in the case of Lehman Brothers

As many remember, and as also frequently mentioned in this book, on 15 September 2008, Lehman Brothers Holdings Inc. filed for Chapter 11 bankruptcy. Evidence presented in the auditor report suggests that insufficient liquidity available was a major factor that led to its default. On September 14, the bank was no longer capable of funding its daily operations due to its clearing bank's collateral claims as it was using most of the available resources to meet intraday liquidity requirements. The bank used several correspondent banks and each ensured an intraday liquidity and credit facility to smooth payment settlement. They increasingly used their available resources to cover intraday and shorter term liquidity requirements; by the end of the first quarter of 2008 these assets amounted to $34 billion and at the third quarter of 2008 they totalled $42 billion. Over time, Lehman used these resources to post with its correspondent banks to ensure intraday payments: when its correspondent banks started reducing the intraday liquidity and credit lines and higher haircuts were applied to tri-party repo collateral, a domino effect triggered larger collateral requirements and some then asked for cash deposits to ensure intraday payments. Towards the end, as more and more of its assets were pledged for intraday payments to correspondent banks, Lehman was left with just $2 billion of available assets and on September 15, when it had a net due outflow of $4.5 billion, it didn't have enough liquid securities and cash available. The bank didn't correctly forecast and assess or estimate the necessary resources for refinancing the intraday payments as this was the most significant element affecting its refinancing capacity asset pool, and it found out just too late that it didn't have sufficient resources.

2.4.9 Some intraday liquidity monitoring indicators

The problems that can arise from intraday liquidity management are not always predictable, and though sophisticated, there may be some elements that can be included in control systems. As the Lehman case showed, there are cases that can hamper sound liquidity management processes in place, including the ones designed to tackle stress conditions. Therefore, forecasting and preparing for possible difficult market conditions will prove very useful. It will prepare the bank's management and address action plans with a preventative focus: this will give precious time for analysis and discussion within the organization that will not be possible to carry out during crisis. There are many factors affecting the usage of intraday liquidity in payment systems and the wider the scope of dedicated controls, the more likely a revealing indicator anticipating problems. Supervisors have also made suggestions for valid intraday liquidity indicators, among these the daily maximum liquidity usage and the available intraday liquidity, both dedicated to intraday needs and overall stock, the total payments carried out in size and numbers and different counterparties (see earlier on in this section on counterparty analysis for intraday liquidity management). Other factors to consider are time-specific and other critical obligations and the value of customer payments made on behalf of financial institution customers. Intraday credit lines extended to financial institution customers and their utilization statistics are also important to verify, along with the timing of intraday payments for the different settlement systems.

An important indicator to monitor is the maximum requirement for intraday liquidity in normal market conditions, calculated as its net cumulative intraday liquidity position over a period of time. The net cumulative intraday liquidity position of a bank is the difference between the value of its payments received and made at any point in the day. The bank's largest negative net cumulative position during the day will show the maximum intraday liquidity requirement on that day, where a positive figure indicates that the bank got more inflows than outflows at a point in time during the day, best calculated on actual settlement times rather than on the posting to the correspondent bank. One way we can use this indicator is to calculate the minimal amount of intraday liquidity requirement to match the largest negative net cumulative position. A positive net cumulative position, a surplus of intraday liquidity available, could occur if it is relying on payments received from other system participants to fund its outgoing payments.

The available intraday liquidity is the amount of intraday liquidity available on a daily basis and in normal market conditions; we will have to monitor the resources available at the beginning of every business day and measure the minimal amount available during the day, according to predefined time intervals.

We should set liquidity management such that it identifies and prioritizes time-specific and other critical obligations in order to meet them when expected; these are obligations that must be settled at a specific time and if we cannot meet these obligations then we will be sanctioned. We then need to identify the volume and value of critical payments and verify they are promptly ensured; we should also keep statistics of the obligations that for some reason fail to be settled, reporting the different anomalies or errors in order to address problems.

Another variable we need to monitor is the value of payments ensured on behalf of customers: as the correspondent bank controls the gross value of daily payments made on behalf of its bank member, it is important we control the value of payments we provide for our customers and we should also have a list of the most relevant ones.

Monitoring the total sum of intraday credit lines granted to financial institution customers is also an important indicator: here the correspondent bank monitors the value of the credit lines used by type extended to the largest five banks, and their maximal daily usage of credit lines granted, by type of line.

The timing of intraday payment, relevant for direct participants, determines the average time of payment settlement through time, and we should monitor whether there are relevant changes to these levels. The indicator is calculated as the value-weighted average time of settlement,

$$\sum (\text{Value}^* \text{Time of settlement})/ \sum \text{Value}$$

Banks can also use the underlying data of timing inflows and outflows to set up stress scenarios that take into account possible changes in the settlement dynamics.

2.4.10 Intraday liquidity stress scenarios

Intraday liquidity requirements and usage of available financial resources can increase significantly during market difficulties, so we should gauge the set stress to quantify the possible impact on the intraday liquidity needs of the changing conditions, looking first at changes in securities' values. The regulators have outlined different types of stress scenarios for intraday liquidity risk: a customer-driven stress where the customer correspondent bank suffers a stress event, forcing the other banks participating in the payment systems to delay payments and so reducing further intraday liquidity available. We also have to assess a market-wide credit or liquidity stress that affects the value of all the assets available for refinancing: this could be a widespread reduction in market value or credit rating of available assets for intraday payments. The indications obtained from these stress testing and scenario analyses need quantifying for the maximal daily liquidity requirement, also measuring the actual residual available intraday liquidity and the possible modification in total payments. We need to distinguish the analysis for the various relevant intraday time periods, we also need to assess the payments ensured on behalf of our own customers and the intraday liquidity and credit lines granted to customers.

2.5 FUNDING CONCENTRATION

Concentrations of funding sources can have a significant impact on liquidity risk as well as systemic implications for the entire banking system. Concentrations in market funding increase liquidity risk. Increased reliance on market funding sources leaves institutions more exposed to the price and credit sensitivities of major fund providers. As a general rule, institutional fund providers are more credit-sensitive and will be less willing than retail customers to provide funds to an institution facing real or perceived financial difficulties. An institution's ability to access capital markets may also be reduced by events not directly related to it. For example, the Asian crisis of 1997 and the collapse of the Russian ruble in 1998 increased volatility and reduced liquidity for various capital market products: following international sanctions on Russia for its Crimea annexation and support to the Ukrainian civil war, it looks like we are now back in a similar situation. Wholesale fund providers will likely refuse to rollover existing funds at institutions whose creditworthiness is (or appears to be) deteriorating. As a result, the institution may find it more difficult to rollover its maturing short-term liabilities, especially any unsecured and uninsured borrowings such as commercial paper. In addition, market funding has an effect on funding costs and profitability, since it is more expensive than traditional core deposit funding.

Concentrations in interbank funding entail contagion risks (see Figure 2.5). Interbank funding can be a volatile funding source, especially in times of crisis, when confidence among institutions is lost and they become reluctant to lend to each other. Concentrations in a few providers of liquidity pose the risk that one significant interbank or wholesale provider will withdraw from the market, or that a large depositor will withdraw large numbers of deposits. Concentrations in secured financing sources pose the risk that funding will not be available at all times or when needed. Institutions that depend too much on securitization may encounter funding difficulties when

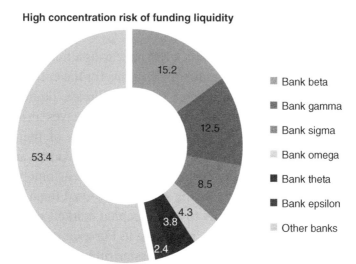

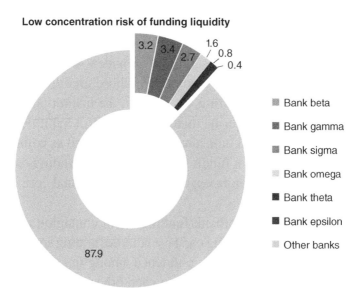

FIGURE 2.5   Cases of high risk of funding liquidity concentration.
Source: The author.

markets are unable to absorb new asset-backed security issues and institutions are forced to hold assets on their books. Possible returns of receivable balances to the balance sheet, as a result of scheduled or early amortization, may result in large asset pools that require balance sheet funding at unexpected or inopportune times. In addition, adverse events in credit markets may result in liquidity and the sudden withdrawal of credit lines granted to asset-backed commercial paper programmes, depleting banks' cash reserves or liquid assets.

Institutions should actively monitor their funding sources to identify potential concentrations, and they should have a well-diversified funding base. Potential concentrations should be understood in a broad sense, encompassing concentrations in terms of providers of liquidity, types of funding (secured vs. unsecured), marketplaces and products, as well as geographic, currency or maturity concentrations.

The specific metric is meant to identify those sources of wholesale funding that are of such significance that withdrawal of this funding could trigger liquidity problems. The metric thus encourages the diversification of funding sources. Key elements to consider in analysing funding concentration are:

- Funding liabilities sourced from each significant counterparty.
- The bank's balance sheet total.
- Funding liabilities sourced from each significant product/ instrument.

Banks and supervisors should monitor both the absolute percentage of the funding exposure and significant increases in concentrations.

2.5.1 Significant counterparties

The numerator for counterparties is calculated by aggregating the total of all types of liabilities to a single counterparty or group of connected or affiliated counterparties, as well as all other direct borrowings, both secured and unsecured, which the bank can determine arise from the same counterparty, such as for overnight CP/CD funding.

A significant counterparty is defined as a single counterparty or group of connected or affiliated counterparties accounting in aggregate for more than 1% of the bank's total balance sheet, although in some cases there may be other defining characteristics based on the funding profile of the bank. A group of connected counterparties is, in this context, defined in the same way as in the Large Exposure regulation of the host country in the case of consolidated reporting for solvency purposes. Intra-group deposits and deposits from related parties should be identified specifically under this metric, regardless of whether the metric is being calculated at a legal entity or group level, due to the potential limitations on intra-group transactions in stressed conditions.

2.5.2 Significant instruments/products

The numerator for the type of instrument/product should be calculated for each individually significant funding instrument/product, as well as by calculating groups of similar types of instruments/products. A significant instrument/product is defined as a single instrument/product or group of similar instruments/products that in aggregate amount to more than 1% of the bank's total balance sheet.

2.5.3 Significant currencies

In order to capture the amount of structural currency mismatch in a bank's assets and liabilities, banks are required to provide a list of the amount of assets and liabilities in each significant currency. A currency is considered significant if the aggregate liabilities denominated in that currency amount to 5% or more of the bank's total liabilities.

2.5.4 Time buckets

The above metrics should be reported separately for the time horizons of less than one month, 1–3 months, 3–6 months, 6–12 months, and for longer than 12 months. In utilizing this metric to determine the extent of funding concentration to a certain counterparty, both the bank and the supervisors must recognize that currently it is not possible to identify the actual funding counterparty for many types of debt. The actual concentration of funding sources, therefore, could likely be higher than this metric indicates. The list of significant counterparties could change frequently, particularly during a crisis. Supervisors should consider the potential for herding behaviour on the part of funding counterparties in the case of an institution-specific problem. In addition, under market-wide stress, multiple funding counterparties and the bank itself may experience concurrent liquidity pressures, making it difficult to sustain funding even if sources appear well diversified.

One must recognize that the existence of bilateral funding transactions may affect the strength of commercial ties and the amount of the net outflow. These do not indicate how difficult it would be to replace funding from any given source. To capture potential foreign exchange risks, the comparison of the amount of assets and liabilities by currency will provide a useful analysis on currency mismatches through swaps, forwards and so on.

2.6 MEASURING ASSET LIQUIDITY

Quoted prices for bonds and other assets acceptable for refinancing as collateral only partially reflect the true value, especially when markets are under strain. This is more likely valid for lower credit rating and less liquid markets, but it can also affect the portfolio of normally liquid securities. There are several factors that we should consider in determining the degree of liquidity of our available assets. Regulators are also addressing the parameters to ascertain and quantify the liquidity levels for the calculation of haircut and LCR, but also for IFRS 13 Fair Value Adjustments and Additional Valuation Adjustments as these need evaluating. Credit spreads versus risk-free curves and bid-ask spreads are the two most important parameters that need controlling and modelling: different levels of credit and bid-ask spreads will set the degree of price certainty. As a result, these will then provide necessary prudential price adjustments in comparison to market quotes (fair value adjustments) but also capital buffers for market uncertainties, close out costs and large positions concentration (additional value adjustments) and the value of our counterbalancing stock. The key variables to measure are therefore the speed of trade execution, the size of transaction, the width of bid-ask spread and bid-ask spread volatility both intraday and end of day, and transaction costs. Applying such liquidity modelling to our asset portfolio, we will be able to identify which are of the best quality for liquidity risk management in times of crisis and which might be affected in terms of market quotes if there's a credit worsening or liquidity conditions deteriorate. For the determination of asset liquidity, we should assess and quantify whether there are sufficient market data available, looking at parameters that in various studies and literature are proving robust liquidity risk measures. Hereafter we will present some useful models to measure liquidity in financial markets. We find some recurrent parameters that apply, these being the dynamic of the bid-ask spreads as a key element to take into account and to be modelled. Bid-ask spread data should be measured during the day, the end of day indication being static and therefore missing important informative power. We also have an interesting element of information from the bid-ask spreads' volatilities, which is best if we can calculate on the intraday data rather than just that at closing.

Another useful and recurrent element is trade volumes for the different financial instruments. The market-maker quotes for different quantities can differ substantially from the actual listed official ones, however: larger sizes or varying market conditions will affect the prices. When analysing traded volumes, we should consider averages, seasonality effects, minima and maxima.

2.6.1 Standard liquidity ratio

A widely applied asset liquidity measurement is what I define here as the standard liquidity ratio (SLR, to distinguish it from the regulatory LCR), and quantifies the asset volume (V) needed for a percentage change price (P):

$$SLR_{it} = \frac{\sum_{t=1}^{T} P_{it} V_{it}}{\sum_{t=1}^{T} |PC_{it}|}$$

In the SLR above, the denominator is the absolute percentage change of the asset price in the time interval considered. The reading is that the greater the SLR, the higher the liquidity of an asset.

The Amihud and Mendelson (1986) model is also useful to determine market liquidity for a specific financial instrument and is based on the average bid-ask spread over a set time interval. Indicated $R_t(j)$ as the average monthly return on an individual portfolio j's asset, in excess of the 90-day return on US Treasury bond, $\beta_t(j)$ is the beta coefficient for j's portfolio, $S_t(j)$ is the average bid-ask spread:

$$R_t(j) = c + \alpha \beta_t(j) + \gamma \log S_t(j)$$

The Amihud and Mendelson (1988, 1991) model-tested results indicate that average portfolio returns are getting higher together with spread.

Amihud, in 2002, proposed a measure for market illiquidity (ILQ), analysing trade volumes and the correlation to liquidity conditions:

$$ILQ^i_T = \frac{1}{D_T} \sum_{t=1}^{D_T} \frac{R^i_{t,T}}{V^i_{t,T}}$$

D_T represents the number of days of data available; R the return on day t for year T; V is the daily volume applied to the same. The day-t impact on the price of one currency unit of volume traded is given by the ratio R/V. This index can give an indicative measure of price dynamics and it is far easier to implement than models relying on bid-ask spreads.

2.6.2 Determining implied spread

A popular and widely used liquidity measure is the one proposed by Roll (1984) where we try to derive the actual spread from the market price time series: the idea is that the return data also include the spread components and therefore we can implicitly calculate it. The Roll approach assumes market efficiency and the same information for the participating counterparties, the spread component we can therefore get from the return series as the trade volume-related one. In order to get the spread element, we need the price series, P_t at closing time t, oscillating between bid and ask quotes that depend on the side originating the trade. We assume that this reproduces the negative serial covariance observed in actual price changes and that the equilibrium price is a random walk process, $V_t = \overline{V} + V_{t-1} + \varepsilon_t$ and the actual market price is $P_t = V_t + \frac{S}{2}Q_t$, the spread being S, constant through time, Q is a variable equal to $+1$ or -1 if the trade is closed at bid or ask price. The change in the price is given by $\Delta P_t = V_t + \frac{S}{2}\Delta Q_t + \varepsilon_t$, if we assume that $cov(\varepsilon_t, \varepsilon_{t-1}) = 0$ (market information efficient) and that buy or sell orders are equally likely

$cov(\Delta P_t, \Delta P_{t-1}) = -1$, we can derive the Roll spread measures in the two equations below, where we get that the more negative the return autocorrelation, the higher the illiquidity:

$$cov(\Delta P_t, \Delta P_{t-1}) = -\frac{s^2}{4}$$

and the serial covariance estimator is obtained:

$$cov = \frac{1}{n} \sum_{t-1}^{n} \Delta P_t \, \Delta P_{t-1} - \overline{\Delta P^2}$$

The last term in the equation is the mean of the ΔP. Roll's measures, given the two assumptions set to obtain it, can be used to determine the implied trades' order spread but cannot be used in the quantification of spreads where the information on market participants is not symmetrical.

Long-Term Balance

Funding liquidity is a risk that arises in the short term but the seeds for this to become a major exposure for a financial institution are spawned in the medium- and long-term strategic management of the interest and refinancing of the bank's balance sheet. Funding liquidity therefore becomes hard to manage in cases where the bank hasn't correctly taken into account the dynamics of deposits, refinancing, asset re-pricing and growth. This third chapter tries to address both the metrics and the risk management elements to consider for a sound long-term balance of assets and liabilities. In the first part we analyse the net stable funding ratio as set by the Basel capital accord and assess the implications and validity for the bank's funding control. In the second, an insight into sight deposits modelling, looking then at the statistical methods and assumptions banks can make on their private customers' behaviours and the reliability of such assumptions in stressed market conditions. The third section then looks at stress testing and scenario analysis for both the assets and liabilities, looking at the impact of such hypotheses on funding liquidity, these being useful to address longer term balance. Lastly, in the fourth section, the size and quality of the securities available for refinancing are analysed, as this is also an element to consider for longer term balancing and liquidity management.

3.1 STRUCTURAL FUNDING

While the very survival of banks is immediately concerned with liquidity crises and day-to-day refinancing, and has been the focus of Chapter 2 on short-term liquidity risk and the securities portfolio set up against unexpected market developments and adverse conditions, or that should be; the structural balance sheet of a bank reflects its willingness to refinance with matching funds assets as well as the market interest rate conditions and, more strategically, its risk appetite and view on spread and liquidity risk. The short term is unquestionably the most immediate commitment and obligation, however this can be somewhat tackled using emergency central bank financing, while the very survival of an institution and its profitability depend on its long-term balance sheet maturity profile – say the disparity or degree of difference between maturing assets and similarly maturing liabilities. This will sound much the same as the traditional ALM discipline and modelling, and indeed it is the very same logic but taken on its liquidity impact: this is the meaning, then, of the net stable funding ratio introduced in the new Basel 3 accord proposal.

The concept of a balance between maturing assets and funding liability isn't new at all, and indeed it is a core element of standard ALM techniques. Here the supervisors have reviewed the weighting and components to be included or excluded from the calculation to improve banks' shock and stress testing assessment and awareness. In the Net Stable Funding Ratio the funding elements are set as the sum of these liability elements:

- Equity and reserve capital, including preferred stock, as long as there is no maturity or this is greater than one year.
- All liabilities with contractual maturities over one year.
- The portion of sight deposits and term deposits with contractual maturities lower than one year but that the bank can prove with strong statistical evidence will stick to the institution

even during extreme market conditions, such as those recently experienced.

■ A part of the interbank money market funding maturing within one year where the bank can demonstrate it will also be kept in stressful market conditions.

In line with the coverage ratio, this coefficient is also intended to be kept by banks at over 100 per cent to ensure a balance of funding sources over investments. It is a calculation to be performed less frequently than the coverage ratio and it should be ensured over time rather than punctually: it is important to ensure stability over time, though it might occur that on some days it could be standing below the minimal level. Another relevant element to keep in mind is related to the ratio's application to the individual legal entity part of a group and the possibility of temporary differences in the ratio between these and the group overall; such a possibility should be discussed and agreed with the various regulators involved.

3.1.1 Determining the available funding

The criterion for funding elements is to consider those over one year and apply the contractual maturity for those expiring in over twelve months or statistical modelling for sight and term deposits. These will then be articulated by regulators into different categories of resilience and for each a weighting factor will be indicated: the products for the different categories will be added. Structural borrowing from central bank lending facilities outside regular open market operations are not to be included in the calculations as this would be misleading and such facilities are intended as a temporary support (it is interesting to assess the treatment of the European Central Bank's long-term financing operations offered to banks).

As explained, the available amount of long-term funding is calculated by assigning the value of equity and other liabilities

TABLE 3.1   Components of stable funding and weighting factors.

Weight	Type of liability
100%	The total amount of capital, including Tier 1 and Tier 2 as defined in existing global capital standards issued by the Basel Committee.
	The total amount of any preferred stock not included in Tier 2 with maturity greater than one year, considering any explicit or embedded options that could reduce it below one year.
	The total amount of secured and unsecured borrowings and liabilities, also including term deposits, with remaining maturities greater than one year and excluding instruments with embedded options reducing them below one year, such as options exercisable at the investor's discretion within one year.
95%	Stable non-maturity sight or term deposits with maturities under one year of retail and small business customers.
90%	Less stable non-maturity deposits and term deposits with maturities below one year by retail and small business clients.
50%	Unsecured money market funding, non-maturity deposits and term deposits under one year, by non-financial corporates, sovereigns, central banks.
	Operational deposits.
	Other funding not included in the categories above, secured or unsecured, maturing within six months to one year, including those from central banks and financial institutions.
0%	All other liabilities not listed in the above categories, including those without a contractual maturity.

Soruce: The author and EBA.

to one of five categories, as presented in Table 3.1. The amount assigned to each category is to be multiplied by a weight (called an ASF factor) and the sum of the weighted amounts will be applied to the ratio.

3.1.2 Required stable funding for assets

Consistent with the approach applied to liabilities, assets with maturity over one year are articulated in groups or categories, multiplied by a scaling factor (the required stable funding factor, RSF). The multiplying factor applied to asset values is to determine the portion of each that requires stable funding from some maturing liability: assets considered by supervisors to be very liquid or available to act for refinancing (repos, central bank and collateral pledge) in stressed market conditions are considered to need lower liquidity for refinancing and will get a lower weight or RSF factor. The weights for the different assets entering the ratio are meant to represent or capture the portion of the bank's balance sheet that would be less liquid and could encounter difficulties being reduced or sold, or could not easily be accepted as collateral, or, more simply, does not have the legal characteristics for such refinancing.

Banks typically rely on sources of secured funding guaranteed by their own assets often in one year, and in these cases they need to verify their own secured issues' maturing profiles. If the bank will receive cash then the weight will be 0%, otherwise if it instead receives another asset, then the weight to that specific asset needs to be used. The assets that are pledged will be weighted in full (100%) unless these return beforehand and within one year.

As per the liabilities, the weights and assets are presented in Table 3.2. We need to take into account that the portion of amortizing loans paying back within the one-year period can be treated as having lower maturity.

Many potential off-balance-sheet exposures do not require direct funding though they can lead to significant liquidity requirements in stressed market conditions: for those of a weight as per the other categories, the liquidity risk regulators deemed it appropriate to address these too; a specific list of assets and weights is presented in Table 3.3.

TABLE 3.2 Asset stable funding weights and categories.

Asset category	Weights
Cash reserves (coins and banknotes), central bank reserves, unencumbered loans to banks subject to prudential supervision with maturity lower than 6 months.	0%
Available, unpledged Level 1 assets	5%
Available, unpledged Level 2A assets	15%
Unencumbered Level 2B assets	50%
HQLA encumbered for a period of 6 to 12 months.	50%
Loans to banks subject to prudential supervision with maturity of 6 to 12 months.	
Deposits with other financial institutions for operational purposes.	
Other assets with a maturity lower than 12 months including loans to non-banks, non-financial corporate customers, retails and SMEs, sovereigns, central banks, public entities.	
Residential mortgages of any maturity that would qualify for the 35% or lower risk weight under the Basel 2 Standardized Approach.	65%
Other loans, excluding loans to financial institutions that would qualify for the 35% or lower risk weight under the Basel 2 Standardized Approach.	
Loans to retail customers and small business customers as defined in the LCR with a maturity under one year, other than those that qualify for the 65% RSF above, excluding those to financial institutions.	85%
Unencumbered securities, including exchange traded equities, that are not defaulted and do not qualify as HQLA.	
Physical traded commodities, including gold.	
All other assets unencumbered for a period of one year or longer.	100%
All other assets not included in the categories listed above.	

Source: The author and EBA.

TABLE 3.3 Off-balance-sheet categories and weights.

Category	Weight
Conditionally revocable and irrevocable credit and liquidity facilities to any client	5% of the undrawn portion
Other contingent funding obligations, including products and instruments such as:	National supervisors can specify the RSF factors based on their national circumstances.

- Unconditionally revocable uncommitted credit and liquidity facilities.
- Guarantees and letters of credit.
- Other trade finance instruments.
- Non-contractual obligations such as potential requests for debt repurchases of the bank's own debt or that of related conduits, securities investment vehicles; structured products where customers anticipate ready marketability, such as adjustable rate notes and variable rate demand notes; managed funds marketed with the objective of maintaining a stable value such as money market mutual funds or other types of stable value collective investment funds.

Source: The author and EBA.

3.2 CUSTOMER DEPOSIT MODELLING

As our discussion is on liquidity funding risk management, we ought to treat to some extent the matter of research on retail customers' deposit stability and its modelling. One can find extensive literature on this topic and it is the subject of dedicated texts. Here we want to present both the regulatory standing and assumptions on deposit stability – the ratios imposed or assumed, and on the other hand the actual impact of depositor behaviours and their actual volatility or change in resilience impact on banks' funding.

Funding through individual customers other than corporate and wholesale markets is a core source of cash inflows for commercial banks. With the exception of pure investment banks, most financial institutions nowadays depend on retail funding. The dynamic of retail funding depends on many factors and is of paramount relevance for the very survival of a bank but also for the new regulatory framework coming into force following the Basel 3 accord (all the new prudential ratios have a core component addressing customer deposit patterns or resilience). Funding through retail or individual non-corporate customers differs substantially from the latter through:

- Typically being of smaller amount.
- Numbering thousands or millions of individual separate accounts.
- Resilience or reluctance to closing or moving the cash.

It is in particular the resilience part that will be addressed here, the pattern or behaviour of customers when it comes to their bank cash and savings funds. As we might observe with our own bank account, we are bound to it through the many habits or services attached to it: our mortgage is provided by the same bank, our credit cards are issued by the same institution, we have banked at the same branch sometimes since we first opened the account when students, house bills are served through standing orders again given to the same bank. In short, changing bank is not an easy and immediate act as would be changing supermarket or holiday destination. The extent to which one customer or millions of customers are loyal or stay with the same bank depends on many factors, amongst these one could list historical time, country, region, personal income, risk awareness and, increasingly, the bank's own reputation or perceived strength (these days one immediately quotes the example of Northern Rock's customers queuing to withdraw their funds; the images broadcast on television of queues waiting their turn to get to the local branch made people think of 1929).

Modelling resilience, often addressed as sight and savings behavioural models, has been studied for decades and can be considered a well-covered and extensively researched field. One can find statistical model types, social or behavioural assumption theories and a combination of the two. Rather than presenting a review of the literature or research on these, we would like to analyse the resilience pattern of such deposits on the banks' liquidity ratios and funding exposure.

Non-maturity deposits, such as sight, current accounts, savings, demand deposits accounts and so on, are a major source of funds for all banks. The characteristic feature of these kinds of deposits is that they have no stated contractual maturity and the balance of these funds can increase or decrease throughout the day without any warning (although in practice the balance is quite stable) as the depositors always have the possibility of adding or withdrawing funds at any time (the embedded options that clients may exercise) at no penalty.

The behaviour of non-maturity deposits reflects rational decision-making on the part of customers based on two factors: received value and perceived value. Higher interest rates paid relative to competitor rates and more consequential barriers to exit create longer term indeterminate maturity deposits. One can often observe that the volume of a non-maturity deposit position fluctuates as clients react to changes in the customer rate and the relative attractiveness of alternative investment opportunities:

- When interest rates rise, the total balance of non-maturity deposits tends to fall as customers become more careful in sweeping their funds into long-term investments to lock up the high level of yields (withdrawal).

■ When interest rates are low, non-maturity deposits become more profitable compared to alternative short-term investments. Their perceived value is the answer to the question of why balances remain on deposit for long periods of time even though the financial advantage is negative. There are cases when clients do not react to changes in the customer rate. Non-maturity deposit funding costs generally demonstrate less volatility than market interest rates. As a result, high non-maturity deposit volumes may actually reduce reprising risk and moderate overall interest rate risk. The cash flow modelling of non-maturing deposits requires dividing deposits into stable and unstable balances.

The stable fraction of the current balance is called the core level and is modelled as a permanent balance (long-term outflows), while the volatile fraction is viewed as overnight money and serves as a buffer for volume fluctuations. As observed in other cases, the results obtained for the value of core deposits vary substantially by institution, depending on the individual bank's supply of deposits and ability to retain deposits. This is important for financial decisions in order to distribute over several years the total value that can be used for investment proposals.

There are many factors to be checked and valued in projecting the future pattern of individual customer deposits. When addressing long-term maturity profiles for funding, outward to five years, one should verify not only the past resilience and the country average statistics, one should also discuss and profile a strategic scenario on interest rate outcomes as well as depositor stability. The liquidity cost component was often underestimated in such sight and savings modelling, as it was mostly the core distribution and rate sensitivity driving the sight's possible time distribution, such that one could sterilize or hedge the rates' forward possible changes upwards or down, by maturity, to lock or stabilize bank commercial spreads.

Indeed the recent crisis has changed the focus and weight for sights and savings funding, it is now more the assurance of maintaining – or the statistical assumptions behind such funding projections – these funds rather than their actual rate sensitivity that is increasingly the focus of greatest attention. The 2009 Greek crisis brought a fundamental change into banking markets that had thus far proved relatively unscathed by financial crises, like Italy or Spain, showing that depositors can actually flee and withdraw money that one considered stable or resilient. Therefore, regulators are correct in asking any bank, irrespective of its past performance or structure, to perform funding deposit stress testing where depositors can leave and can do so in a relatively short time (30 days or 90 days; whether there is a definitively correct countdown is unsure and depends on the gravity, intensity and the specific crisis and country affected, still it might well be very fast, as the Spanish case proved, with billions of sight and savings retail deposits being sent abroad to safer countries like Germany or Holland).

3.2.1 Regulatory approaches on deposit stability

Driven by experience of cases of sudden customer withdrawal, the regulators imposed in the Basel 3 standards a tight stability coefficient, as discussed in the stress testing and liquidity coverage ratios. These assumptions fall short of specific valuation both on the historical depositor behaviours and on the differences across countries. The rationale is to ensure the central banks and governments have sufficient certainty that the banks are not overly leveraging the deposit base, as ultimately the assurance on deposit guarantee falls on them. So, rather than being accurate in modelling, the drive has been more likely a conservative assessment. As the crisis has shown, historical patterns prove quite dubious and easily fail once the concrete risk of banks not being able to meet their obligations and ensure payments spreads. Any assumption in such circumstances might be generous, as we saw in the case of Greek depositors and then Spanish. The real question then is the role of central banks in assuring deposit payments and in their surveillance. The possibility, therefore, that such stringent assumptions on depositors will prevent a crisis remains to be proven. Indeed, it is more likely to penalize bank profitability and the possibility of ensuring convenient financing to the economy, as the cost of liquidity buffers will translate into either higher spreads to customers or reluctance to lend per se on the corporate customer side. The experience is a two-sided story, one where corporate customers, primarily the financial institutions accessing the provisioning markets on a daily basis, have the first impression and evidence of other banks' difficulties. This will anticipate private depositors and, in the form of reduced lending, will rapidly drain corporate liquidity. The regulators have addressed this correctly. The second aspect, more related to costs and crisis length and peculiarity, results in likely increased facilities amongst institutions with similar problems at times of drained money market flows.

3.2.2 Depositor behaviours

The government deposits insurance protection scheme is assured typically for private individuals. We mentioned corporate behaviour and predictable reactions when crises or difficulties in the markets loom, more rapidly averting or shifting sums or hampering lending. The case is quite substantially different for private customers, here generically addressed though major differences will be seen for affluent private banking depositors, typically assuring millions of base sums, and the more general mass market depositors. The affluent will be better informed and tend to be investing in a more sophisticated product range than plain sight or term deposits. They are also more likely to be fleeing rapidly like corporate deposits, therefore addressing these inflows differently from the mass market one is quite correct. Mass market depositors span students to pensioners, throughout the general population. They will likely be with one bank, rather than multiple relations as might be seen for corporate and affluent customers. In many countries, especially those where there have been few or no bank runs or large banking failures that have led to depositor losses, the trust in governments and central banks ensures stability for mass funds. Thus, the very first analysis the liquidity risk manager ought to perform is a country-specific assessment of previous crises and banking stability, central bank intervention and media standing. An aspect often left aside or unmentioned is the government's capacity to drive communication or, put differently, the influence on media, as mass markets' trust in institutions when it comes to banking deposits depends largely on this perception, panic often leading to irrational actions. Contingency plans then should be drafted both at individual bank but also at regulatory level. We can see in Figure 3.1 the historical levels of a bank's sight items (the data presented are in billions of euros).

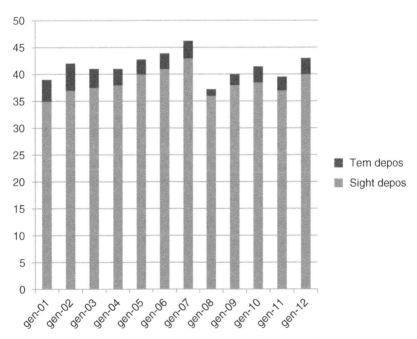

FIGURE 3.1   A bank's exemplificative deposits evolution.
Source: The author.

Historical variations might depend on several different factors, like for example central bank inflation targets or the monetary base, the economic cycle, etc.

The increased relevance of internet accounts and therefore the facility to open, close or transfer across banks is changing mass depositor behaviours, and these are adding speed and volatility to a large chunk of small accounts. They ought to be monitored, statistics of sudden or unusual patterns analysed and discussed at managerial level when likely experienced during liquidity crises, and should be regularly presented to group strategic committees, such as the group Alco. Accounts that are just offered online with special conditions or features in terms of remuneration should indeed be kept separate from traditional ones.

Communication is the main trust and stability driver, news with a negative outlook on the institution affects deposit behaviour; information coming from penalties of any kind, operational problems and frauds, senior management reputation, rating agencies' assessment and updated releases, and quarterly reports are all important elements that may affect the reputation and perception of a bank's soundness.

3.2.3 Modelling assumptions and impacts on funding costs

Given that it isn't the intent herein to address the mathematical modelling and statistical assumptions of any deposit stability (sight and savings viscosity), we shall analyse the possible impact on funding of such assumptions. There are different degrees of sophistication and complexity in modelling resilience or stability over time of mass customer deposits. The first question and assumption relates to the estimate of the portion at any given time of the percentage of deposits that are stable, though they legally and contractually can be withdrawn at any time. Apart from risk aversion and a regulatory prudential stance, as indicated before the consumer attitude towards banking and deposits can change rapidly and is also affected by changes in spending patterns, strong seasonality factors and demographic factors. All of these elements assume that a significant portion of deposits at sight or short term is indeed renewed and maintained at banks as times goes by. It is also worth noting that inflationary rates will have a dramatic impact on the modelling. The second aspect to assess is the supposed forward maturity; again, these have to be consistent to banks' set risk appetite and structural balance sheet's interest rates exposure. The longer the estimated maturity and the larger the portion of sights and short-term deposits assumed stable, the greater the impact of yield curve shifts of the balance sheet. In brief, the greater the willingness to believe and trust the stability and validity of such models, the more likely the balance sheet merits management intervention accordingly. I deem a cautious approach preferable, there being too many variables and elements that might in the medium term invalidate hedging taken. Non-maturity deposits have a few common characteristics:

- Account holders can add and subtract balances at any time without costs.
- There is no specific maturity.
- The interest rate of these accounts usually follows the open market interest rate.
- The stock usually changes in response to changes in the open market interest rate.

Evaluating the mark-to-market value of non-maturity deposits is difficult. However, it is important information when evaluating the bank's exposure to interest rate risk. Theoretically, the maturity, duration and interest rate risk are zero because the assets can be withdrawn at any time at their face value. This means that they do not have an effect on the bank's interest rate risk at all. In practice, the opposite is true. The difference between the interest rate of the non-maturity deposit and the market rate varies the most when compared to other deposits.

Banks generally make three different assumptions about the rate indexation and maturity of non-maturity deposits. For example, the bank may consider them fully rate sensitive and as short maturity because the bank may at any time elect to change the rates paid on those funds. Other banks consider these to be fixed-rate funds with longer maturities because management only rarely changes the rate paid on the deposits. An alternative view to non-maturity deposits is to view them as products with embedded options whose maturity or rate indexation will depend on the behaviour of customers and competitors and the pricing policies of bank management. The assumption of embedded options implies that management's view of the maturity and rate indexation can change with the interest rate.

Non-maturity deposit rates are usually much lower than market interest rates. Moreover, the interest rate earned on these accounts is usually market-driven but with various paces of adjustment. In some cases, the interest rate is near zero while some savings accounts have interest rates set at a notional level with low correlation to market interest rates. The deposit rates for some accounts tend to be also somewhat discrete. Furthermore, the general market competition has an impact on the bank's pricing behaviour.

There is also empirical evidence that the total funds in non-maturity deposits move in response to changes in market interest rates. The general interest rate level has an impact on the customer behaviour, because the customer's opportunity cost increases with interest rates. In practice, a holder's objective is to keep a minimum positive balance in their account to be able to meet their liquidity or short-term savings needs. Usually, when market rates increase, holders tend to keep their current accounts at their minimum balance and transfer unnecessary money to more profitable assets. In contrast, when market interest rates decrease, customers are likely to keep their savings in current accounts. This implies that the stock of deposits might also respond asymmetrically to market rate changes. In particular, this is the case when the deposit interest rate is reviewed rarely or is fixed forever. The sensitivity of deposit stock to market interest rates is a relevant source of interest rate risk and should be taken into consideration when planning a hedging strategy.

3.2.4 Dynamic regression models

We can further explore demand deposit modelling and assumptions, as they are such a key element in liquidity management. The literature here is ample and consolidated, some references are listed in the bibliography and many more can be found easily through a web search. I am mentioning here just one: the Jarrow and van Deventer (1998) dynamic regression sight deposit mechanism. The authors link the demand deposit rates to the domestic banking market dynamics (these are the beta factors in the equation below) and to the actual interest rate levels (r):

$$i(t) = i(t-1) + \beta_0 + \beta_1 r(t) + \beta_2(r(t) - r(t-1))$$

where the change in the demand deposit rate is a function of both the level of market rates (r) and of the β_0, β_1 and β_2 that are the domestic sight deposit market characteristics (e.g. the degree of banking sector concentration, private customer loyalty, internet banking development/penetration); Jarrow and van Deventer imply serial correlation to be one.

In order to take into account varying interest rates on non-maturity demand deposits versus treasury securities, Jarrow and van Deventer make the assumptions (I deem pretty simplified but still reasonable) that we have two types of buyers/sellers in the non-maturity demand deposit market: banks and financial institutions and private investors. Jarrow and van Deventer assume here that there are relevant restrictions in force and some mobility resistance in the demand deposit markets (e.g. historical fidelization towards banks; marketing, residential mortgage clauses imposing current accounts to be kept at the financing bank, indirect account closing costs like changing billing address or issuing a new credit card). On the financial operators' side, it is the trading experience, the wholesale customer bases, expensive technological requirements and regulatory capital that constitute the constraints/barriers in competing with banks. This entails that only few banks access the demand deposit markets;

individual investors do not have such limitations. Jarrow and van
Deventer also assume that private investors and banks have the possibility of getting liquid treasury securities and that short selling is
possible for both.

Jarrow and van Deventer assume that zero-coupon bonds are
freely traded and so are money market accounts, and that the return of
a money market account is aligned to the shortest maturing treasury
bond and this will distinguish it from a demand deposit. We can then
determine the risk-free interest spot rate, $r(t)$, as follows:

$$r(t) = \frac{1}{P(t, t+1)} - 1$$

where $P(t,T)$ is the zero-coupon bond reimbursing at maturity T, with
the price at time t. Then the value of the money market account (B)
can be obtained by rolling the shortest maturity zero-coupon bond
over:

$$B(t) = B(t-1)(1 + r(t-1)), \text{ where } B(0) = 1$$

The Jarrow and van Deventer model assumes that there are only a
limited number of banks and that these can issue demand deposits
with a periodic rate $i(t)$ and that the costs are included in the rate
$i(t)$. It is assumed that demand deposits are floating-rate instruments
paying $i(t)$, net of administrative expenses.

Jarrow and van Deventer show that a demand deposit for banks
can also be presented as an interest rate swap, where the principal
is dependent on past market rates and deposits are considered as
non-defaulting instruments. The net present value of such a swap
will then be:

$$V(0) = D(0) + E\left(\sum_{t=0}^{\tau-2} \frac{D(t+1) - D(t)}{B(t+1)}\right) - E_0\left(\frac{D(\tau-1)}{B(\tau)}\right)$$

$$- E_0\left(\sum_{t=0}^{\tau-1} \frac{i(t)D(t)}{B(t+1)}\right)$$

Here, $V(0)$ is the net present value of demand deposit from time 0 to time τ, calculated as an initial deposit at $D(0)$ plus the changes over time. It is netted of the return of the $\tau -1$ deposit at time τ and of the present value of administrative costs.

The net present value is an estimate of the bank return from issuing demand deposits. The equation can also be expressed as:

$$V(0) = E_0 \left(\sum_{t=0}^{\tau} \frac{D(t)(r(t) - i(t))}{B(t - 1)} \right)$$

This being the discounted cash flows from investing $D(t)$ into short-term investment and receiving $r(t)$ at a cost of $i(t)$ each time. At time $t+1$ the payment of $D(t)[r(t) - i(t)]$ is assured. This is like an interest rate swap maturing after τ periods, where one gets floating at $r(t)$ and is paying floating at $i(t)$ and an amortizing/expanding principal of $D(t)$ at t.

This can also be applied to identify the optimal hedging for demand: Jarrow and van Deventer would then be going long on the shortest bond with $D(0)$ and shorting the interest rate swap. We can also add the reserve requirements to the model:

$$V(0) = E_0 \left(\sum_{t=0}^{\tau-1} \frac{D(t)(1 - m)(r(t) - i(t))}{B(t - 1)} \right)$$

Where reserve requirements are $(1 - m)r(t)$ and the interest paid $i(t)$ is the funds the bank must hold against specified deposit as per the national regulation in force.

3.3 STRESS TESTING AND SCENARIO ANALYSIS

As applied to banks, stress testing is the assessment of their liquidity position and changes in the risk exposure when we assume severe market conditions. Stress testing is necessary to support strategic decision making and to set aside the necessary prudential financing means. The term stress testing also often refers to the analysis and specific tests that take into account the potential impact of severe but still plausible changes in the macroeconomic and financial market conditions.

Stress testing can be performed to assess whether there are adequate financial resources, valid processes, limits or IT systems. Liquidity stress testing will need to ascertain that our liquidity management and controls system are capable of enduring market and economic shocks. Liquidity stress testing needs to verify the validity first of the governance and control systems. We should also evaluate our contingency and emergency plans (see Chapter 5). It is also important to test the validity of the liquidity risk measurement methodologies in place and check the changes on risk calculations. Further, we need a stress testing analysis performed before new systems and procedures or products are released, considering the liquidity risk component explicitly and as a separate element.

Scenario analysis further completes the stress testing: these are ad hoc analyses where custom designed shocks or changes in market parameters are tested and results analysed to gauge systems or limits or other relevant variables.

3.3.1 Using stress testing to improve banks' own risk governance

The role of the board and senior management once again is crucial in the stress testing framework: it needs to take into account the indications provided in the liquidity risk governance framework (including control, contingency funding plan and stock of high quality liquid assets). Liquidity risk control is expected to present to the board and senior management the results of the stress testing and a suggested action plan derived from this. The objectives and specific relevant scenarios should also be indicated from the senior management, the company's board should proactively discuss the results of the analysis and the strategic implications.

Experience clearly shows that the more articulated the stress testing analysis and the senior management involvement in the discussion, the more likely the company will be able to cope with sudden changes in market conditions. The stress testing analysis should also be subject to regular thorough review so that it is itself experiencing a re-assessment (often this is not done or it is performed rarely, providing eventually a pretty meaningless analysis).

The involvement of the company's board eventually becomes necessary not just for the required formal awareness of potential risk exposures but also to ensure the necessary investments are granted budgets and the strategy case is reviewed and implemented (thus the necessity of such a high-level sharing process). Unfortunately, it is the problematic and unwanted that emerges from stress testing analysis, and as it is very complicated to prevent or get ready for such rare or extreme events, the management will be facing tough strategic impacts and decision processes.

3.3.2 Liquidity stress testing rationale

Many financial crises have shown, especially when it comes to liquidity risk, that banks in general are not adequately prepared (though some are). An important factor is that the stress testing or emergency and scenario shocks were not adequate or, in most cases, did not serve their purpose. It is fundamental, apart from the validity and logic applied in performing stress testing, that the results and the rationales do not remain as an isolated analysis or confined to a reporting process: we should make sure the stress testing results are an integral part of the company's strategic decision-making process. We should ensure that there is an active discussion amongst the senior management on the results presented and that the analysis is regularly challenged. We should seek feedback from the various divisions and businesses most affected and those that apparently are unscathed.

A common perceived weakness or reason for the ineffectiveness of stress testing analysis is related to the extreme and, at times, completely unrealistic events considered: in short, the exercise was totally hypothetical and lacked the critical feedback of the relevant functions involved, it was a kind of sterile reporting process. Stress testing can also be of no advantage if, though well designed and carried out, it remains an additional reporting factor that is never challenged nor reviewed and no decisions ever follow from it. This actually is an indicator to be monitored: if no decisions nor review are taken from the analysis results, then its set-up and content must be changed, but it might even be necessary to rethink the whole internal process. We might experience improvements through adding some new elements to the analysis (changes should be quite frequent in the set-up and the parameters applied) or forcing some decision making as routine following its presentation to the relevant risk committee or the board.

Both the regulators and best practice envisage a change in approach for the different stress tests performed within banks, moving forward from single risks and stand-alone analysis (e.g. single business line or legal entity testing) and implementing instead wider, group or cross-risk types and divisions analysis. This will improve correlation impact analysis and unexpected decoupling assessments, possibly identifying unconventional situations that one could measure. It is the case that devoting time and effort to regularly challenging and improving these analyses will likely result in more experienced checks and valuable results.

Another valuable lesson learnt is that stress testing was not sufficiently flexible to market, political and economic condition changes (e.g. difficulties in combining, new scenarios or parameter setting). We should ensure, then, that there are adequate budgeted investments dedicated to stress testing analysis so that databases and calculation engines permit flexibility on portfolios and parameters, as well as different frequencies including intraday if needed. The test complexity can vary significantly as we may have single-factor analysis to very articulated multi-factor analysis. There may be additional analyses to assess the impact of stressed macroeconomic changes to earnings or credit quality.

We need to address stress testing data requirements and ensure there is adequate availability in terms of timing and completeness. It might be a substantial challenge for the largest financial institutions with multi-country operations: data might differ across different legal entities and could be difficult to transfer consistently. In this book we have not reserved a dedicated section to data quality and the possibilities for enhancing – other than via improved technology – the information set available: I am of the opinion that the problems related to technology are unfortunately not the first and major obstacle to the limitations that hamper banks, as the greatest obstacles typically come from within the organization where there isn't a strong and systematic habit to challenge the information presented in reporting. At lower and higher managerial levels it is not common to ask the source, the date of closing consistency, the parameters and assumptions made in the data reported. If such a practice was regularly applied, the operational and qualitative limitations would then be addressed in a timely fashion and, in brief, the technology teams would have far greater time to sort out weaknesses and problems rather than rushing in at the last minute. It is also a matter of openly sharing across divisions problems and limitations in the analysis, this would also focus attention on data quality over time.

Another important factor to be considered in stress testing analysis is that banks' risk models and pricing tools rely mostly (or solely) on backward-looking historical time series. This unfortunately is not sufficient for predicting problems, as time series suffer additionally with the further limitation that the relations or correlations amongst risk factors are not necessarily identifiable from historical patterns and might change structurally. There is also a complexity in weighting the historical time series shock phases and data, some disruptive ones or anomalies can last for limited periods and be outweighed by long time frames or perceived inadequately: deviating reactions occur suddenly and might be relatively short lived, then normality or structural new conditions can emerge. Indeed, financial market history helps and is needed, but a valid stress-testing programme nowadays cannot solely be structured on time series analysis and requires careful forecasting add ons. This implies that the stress testing model cannot be a pure quantitative application and needs qualitative judgement inputs. In sharing the results and validation of the stress testing methodology, the regulator and internal functions involved must challenge purely quantitative approaches and be wary of the assumptions made in developing the programmes.

Another mistaken or questionable approach to stress testing modelling is to assume financial products, especially those where the market prices are less liquid and infrequent and the derivatives over the counter are designed ad hoc for few clients, behave somehow similarly to other financial products with similar features: here, too, the recent crisis and abnormal conditions proved these assumptions were not applicable.

Specific risks for liquidity funding should be taken into account in stress testing programmes, like the possibilities, for example, of a company always being in a position to issue own debt, or able to raise funds at relatively stable spreads. We need instead to challenge these hypotheses and include in the stress testing additional possible requirements in terms of collateral posting in cases of multiple credit notch downgrading on the counterparty credit risk exposure or on the derivative hedging in place. The derivative positions will require carefully designed analysis, as these are the most likely to be affected in cases of financial crisis; liquidity needs to be assessed.

We should also consider within the stress analysis the possible effect on perceived market reputation, with a focus on risks from off-balance-sheet vehicles, and we should carefully assess specifically the risks associated with commitments to structured credit securities, including the case that assets will need to be taken on the balance sheet for reputational reasons. Both for funding liquidity and other risk types, there are important stress testing activities that need to be performed to ensure the validity of stress analysis through time, such as regularly assessing assumptions and striving for forward-looking adjustments that consider the evolution of market conditions or might anticipate it. For new financial products or new activities and markets, the assessment needs to be granular and the stress testing regularly performed before these are authorized and undertaken. Another important element, as seen before, and a weakness in much stress testing, was the expected time period for shock and impact in the simulation: we need to consider several different time periods in the analysis.

3.3.3 Improving controls

So far the rationale to perform stress testing has been to forecast or identify risk exposure that hasn't emerged from standard analysis and to prepare the banks to manage the unforeseen impact of a crisis or problems. Another important purpose of such stress analysis is to help the identification or the ongoing improvement of control process design. The results of granular testing, if well set up and performed regularly, will present indications for better controls in the product pricing and modelling, in the distribution process, or in the contingency liquidity planning or in the execution processes, and so on. From this feedback is likely to flow data for developing newer and better types of analysis: a kind of learning process where the organization can grow and enhance performance from within, and this will need to be articulated for the various businesses in the bank, in particular the more operational ones.

3.3.4 Stress testing methodology

The impact of stress tests is usually evaluated against one or more models. The particular measures used will depend on the specific purpose of the stress test, the risks and portfolios being analysed and the particular issue under examination. A range of measures may be needed to determine an adequate valuation of the impact. Typical measures that can be used to carry out the liquidity stress test assessment are high-quality liquid asset values, profit and loss, available capital or risk-weighted assets, liquidity and funding gaps. In order to effectively challenge the business model and support the decision-making process, the analysis has to assess the nature of linked risks across portfolios and across time. A relevant aspect in this regard is the role played by liquidity conditions for determining the ultimate impact of a stress test.

Stress testing should cover a range of outcomes, especially forward-looking ones, and aim to take into account system-wide interactions and feedback effects. An effective stress test should comprise a spectrum of different events, internal and external, and have a range of severity levels, so as to understand possible vulnerabilities and the effect of nonlinear risks. These forward-looking outcomes should include changes in portfolio risk exposures that are not already part of the historical risk dataset: these can be obtained from the contribution and expert analysts.

It can be helpful to conduct a stress programme including several factors at the same time, because simply testing factors individually may not reveal their potential interaction, particularly if that interaction is complex and not intuitively understandable. Sensitivity and event analysis has additional benefits in helping to reveal whether quantitative approaches are working as imagined. For example, one can check the assumption that a relationship continues to be linear when extreme inputs are used. If the analysis results show that a certain model is unstable or does not work as originally foreseen with extreme inputs, then we should rethink the model or change certain parameters or weights.

3.3.5 Reverse stress testing

A stress test should also determine what events could challenge the survival of the bank and possibly spot hidden risks and interactions amongst these. In line with individual bank characteristics, such stress tests should span the relevant business areas and include the events that are considered very damaging. As part of the overall stress testing assessment, it is important to include some extreme scenarios that would cause the firm to become insolvent. We can also perform a stress test starting from the result of another stress analysis and then try to identify and list what events could possibly have produced such an outcome. As part of an overall stress test, a bank should aim to take account of simultaneous pressures in funding and asset markets, and the impact of a reduction in market liquidity on exposure valuation. Funding and asset markets may be strongly interrelated, particularly during periods of stress. We can enrich stress testing analysis by considering interrelations between many factors.

The effectiveness of risk mitigation techniques should be regularly challenged and stress testing should facilitate the development of risk mitigation or contingency plans for different cases. Banks can enhance their stress analysis by considering highly leveraged counterparties and their implicit vulnerability to specific asset classes or market movements, assessing also the wrong-way risk for collateral and underlying related assets. We may have large gross exposures to leveraged counterparties like hedge funds or investment banks that may be particularly exposed to specific asset types or market movements. Typically these exposures are completely secured by posted collateral and margining agreements: these exposures may increase at once and have potential cross-correlation of credit risk and negative correlation.

According to Basel 3, stress scenarios can use a minimum of four time horizons including an overnight, a 30-day, a 90-day and a one-year time horizon and one may be required to use more time horizons where necessary to reflect capital structure, risk profile, complexity, activities, size and other risk factors.

3.3.6 Scenario analysis

Scenario analysis and stress testing are often used and understood as being synonymous. It can also be the case that stress testing combines scenario analysis and therefore the two terms are indeed the same exercise. I think that the correct difference between the two relates to the building logic behind each. The stress test covers an extreme shock to a relevant variable, to some extent this could even be uncorrelated to the historical level: the indications so far have been to be carefully assessing risk factors' time series, relevance and duration, considering shocks that might not necessarily have occurred in the past – in magnitude or perseverance – and analysing the credibility and indications of results. Reverse stress was also a suggestion, identifying the possible conditions (of markets or controls) that could have produced such results.

Scenarios are a more qualitative exercise, not necessarily searching for extreme events or radical shocks that are considered applicable or, to some extent, could occur in reality. In short, while stress testing is meant to assess the banks in cases of plausible but still rare events, we shall consider instead the scenario as more of a more likely event review that considers or might include some peculiar or infrequent situations but it might well occur in the ordinary future of the organization. Stress testing might never occur, instead a combined analysis of scenario and stress testing may enhance the capacity of an organization to predict and manage unforeseen situations. As said, most bank stress tests were not designed to capture the extreme market events that were experienced, some factors in the stress tests did not follow real cases as these developed. Stress programmes tended to reflect milder shocks and assume shorter durations; it was clear that there were correlations in portfolio positions, risk factors and markets in cases of systemic crisis.

Banks have many techniques to build scenarios, usually these first result from feedback and the indications of experienced analysts and management. The inputs are then put to work starting from some event, internal or external, and from there tuned to the specific factors or processes we want to assess. For funding liquidity, the cash flow projections, broken down by product and customer, should be structured in the scenario and stress testing combined analysis: specific changes to customers and groups of clients' behaviour, simultaneous and partially aligned negative impact on collateral posting on derivative obligations and variations of credit rating of some counterparties. Listing these factors, the complexity behind a credible and sound exercise emerges at once:

- We need timely and complete datasets, validated and recognized by involved functions (this might not be taken for granted, as accounting and managerial data often differ significantly, as does risk and business information).
- Multiple factor relations cannot be calculated and implemented immediately, especially if we do not have sufficient historical information available.
- Extreme shocks or wide ones do not follow a recipe, we need to understand what is the credible and logical threshold/level, this needs discussion and above all good understanding of markets and their complexity.
- The perimeter is also an important element to identify, checking the whole bank/group or single country or legal entity might give a very different result and validity in terms of decision-making.

A good approach is to combine many scenarios together with stress testing of some key market parameters; also, it is worth grouping differently business lines or subsidiaries or portions of risk factors. The wider the scope and the variety of scenarios and parameters, the more interesting and likely useful the results, but also the complexity in calculation and feedback gathering.

A way to approach funding liquidity scenario analysis is to use liquidity at risk models (see Chapter 4) and combine results qualitatively into the structured stress testing after feedback from experienced analysts on the results.

We should look at liquidity in the money markets and varying conditions with scenario analysis, assuming a variety of cases and hypotheses, ideally reviewing these regularly with the bank's treasury.

3.3.7 Internal capital and stress testing

In order to ensure financial stability, supervisors pay attention not only to the single bank level of liquidity risk, but also the risks that any large single institution poses to the financial markets, particularly relevant for companies are larger international organizations that have a large share in terms of volumes, transactions and participation to payments and settlement systems.

It follows, then, that stress testing will be an integral component in the internal capital adequacy assessment process (ICAAP) for bank self-assessment of risk exposure and capital requirement, to ensure sustainability. Stress tests should also be used in regulatory discussions on capital adequacy assessments. Bank risk managers nowadays are aware of both the importance for regulators of stress testing and also of the ICAAP process: the two must be a live process and cannot be limited to a summary document or reporting to senior management and the board of directors. The ICAAP should include a stress testing indication and the corrective measures resulting must be indicated. The disclosure on stress testing results will then be an increasing part of the process: I expect rating agencies and the market to also require disclosure.

CHAPTER 4

Liquidity Value At Risk

This fourth chapter deals with a matter requiring a dedicated book, separate from funding liquidity risk, and it is for this reason the shortest. For completion, a brief insight on the separate topic of liquidity risk, the value of risk modelling considering liquidity effects in the prices of securities, has been included. The first section introduces models and estimations for security liquidation timelines in market risk measures. The second presents the market liquidity adjusted risk modelling approach to adjust for various securities' different levels of liquidity.

4.1 MARKET LIQUIDITY EFFECTS

In the context of market risk, liquidity is the risk resulting from being unable to dispose of securities and positions at a reasonable cost and in due length of time, these being the trade-off costs of the immediate disposal and the risk of keeping the position. The costs will largely depend on the size of the position compared to the normal market size of the transaction and security type, these varying from extremely liquid to the opposite extreme.

4.1.1 Market volatility

The price volatility measured from the opening time to the closing is typically significantly higher than the volatility taken from one closing to the next.

Infrequently traded stocks are characterized by large bid-ask spreads, conversely extremely liquid bonds, such as US Treasuries, are traded in small size and thin bid-ask ranges. The breadth of the spread depends on market supply and demand size for any specific security at a precise time: it varies depending on the securities, on the demand and supply at the time of quotation and on the markets' appetite for specific types of security. The type of order and its execution will drive the bid-ask spread. We can list different types of market orders:

- A market order that can be filled at market or prevailing price.
- A limited order when one sets a limit to sell or buy securities at a given level or better.
- A day order is applicable for a specified trading day then is cancelled.
- A fill or kill must be executed immediately and in its entirety or not at all.
- A stop order that applies when the security passes a certain price level.

The bid-ask spread is essentially a negotiation in progress and, to be successful, traders must be willing to take a stand and walk away in the bid-ask process through limit orders.

4.2 MARKET LIQUIDITY VALUE AT RISK

The financial market developments described above have reinforced the interaction between funding liquidity risk and market liquidity risk. This has consequences for the management of liquidity risk.

The strong link between funding liquidity risk and market liquidity risk is closely related to the move towards the originate-to-distribute model of banking. This is a sophisticated mechanism that relies on complex products, liquid markets and a large number of operators to allocate risk efficiently. The shift to such a model places greater importance on the interaction of funding and market liquidity, particularly in stressed market conditions. The difficulty with this model is that products may be opaque, market liquidity may dry up, and some operators may have opposing incentives. Thus this model leads to a number of risks intrinsic to its mechanism or linked more generally to the greater interdependence of the financial system.

Banks' treasuries keep asset stocks available for repo or actual disposal for normal financing needs and additional stocks in case of strained funding conditions. The liquidity of the various assets kept for financing will vary depending on the type of asset, and these will also change over time. While some assets will maintain high liquidity in complex market conditions, others will prove to be far more difficult to use in times of market stress. The quantity also affects the asset's liquidity, as trying to dispose of large quantities of less liquid assets may trigger additional market illiquidity and further increase the difficulties in disposing of the assets and getting the funds needed. Indeed, in most market conditions, the sale of the assets may not even be feasible at all if not through a private transaction rather than through the market. Funding difficulties may also relate to credit market conditions, and then a bank cannot ensure a loan nor securitize loan portfolios.

If liquidity funding is hampered, we might be forced to sell at once securities or more valuable assets, thus experiencing losses and so weakening results and the capital base. Often, the effects are exponential and can result in a spiral loop where the attempts to sell assets can further limit market liquidity and so also affect other banks' liquidity facilities. This could lead to an overall decrease in prices caused by such a large disposal all at once and thus reduce the funding capacity for all the owners of such securities. In turn, this might affect the prices of similar or related securities and will put pressure across the financial market as a whole. As a result, the banks might seek secured interbank lending so as not to have to dispose of the assets, but this might be hampered by credit risk concern: usually market difficulties will reduce credit line availability. Hence the domino effect: market and funding liquidity conditions can be amplifying, leading to liquidity bottlenecks and, as we know when analysing the effects of reputation on depositors' stability, confidence plays an important role in trust in a bank and this is of even greater relevance in the wholesale financial markets.

So market and funding liquidity variations are fundamental to predicting looming financial crises, as these two risks are linked and the potential systemic consequences of liquidity shortages are inevitably affected by asset valuations. Globalization of financial markets has also increased the risk of contagion across countries. The set of these time series shows that funding and market liquidity correlation becomes stronger as financial markets worsen. An important element to consider is the hypothesis of asset prices in normal market conditions and in particular those regarding the correlations among assets and securities: these can alter during a financial crisis, leading to a very different correlation structure. Avalanche effects and fear of contagion can lead to correlation anomalies (if compared to normal market conditions). Quite interestingly, there is evidence that funding liquidity will also modify liquidity of prices for largely volume traded assets like government bonds.

We can identify three distinct relations of funding and market liquidity. One occurs when the reduced market liquidity is also reducing the funding capacity of the bank through these assets. Another is related to the volatility of prices as a result of higher haircuts and margin calls applied in repos and associated refinancing transactions. In addition, higher volatility for derivatives trades will affect the collateral requirements: banks will have to increase posting and this will affect their overall available resources for refinancing.

Market risk arises from the changes in level or volatility of asset/security prices. Typically, mid-prices of bid/offer are used for the Value at Risk (VaR) evaluation, though this needs to be adjusted at the time of sale (liquidation) as it will be carried out not at the mid but at the lower bid price. In addition, size and time affect the bid price level itself. The actual price at which the transaction will be executed varies as the size and speed of the transaction affects the bid-ask spread. It also will vary depending on the width of the spread. These elements indicate that VaR needs to reflect these liquidation factors in order to provide for liquidity risk measurement. It is therefore necessary to take into account liquidity risk in the VaR measurement as in circumstances such as those described so far, standard VaR models will lead to inaccurate or inadequate results, including likely underestimation of exposure: the appropriate measurement will lead to severe limit breaches and escalation being triggered.

VaR adjusted for liquidity risk has been studied extensively – the bibliography lists some works, the literature being vast and evolving rapidly. There are a number of studies that are devoted to incorporation of liquidity risk into market risk VaR measurements; once a model is estimated then we have to verify its accuracy and validity, performing back-testing analysis and therefore comparing the results for standard VaR measures and VaR inclusive of liquidity risk.

In order to measure the market liquidity cost or price for any security, the actual executed traded price of an asset could be compared to the middle of the bid-ask spread at the time of execution, the liquidity costs can be measured as a percentage of the mid-price for a quantity q at time t, $L_t(q)$ function of trading fees $F(q)$, the price impact costs PI and the delay costs D in the executions:

$$L_t(q) = F(q) + PI_t(q) + D_t(q)$$

$F(q)$ are transaction fees and commissions, $PI_t(q)$ are price impact costs for a q size transaction calculated as the difference between transaction price and the middle of the bid-ask spread. The $D_t(q)$ are costs incurred if a position cannot be immediately duly closed out. The direct trading costs are normally of limited relevance for most investors, especially in the wholesale market and for professional investors, while the delay costs are normally also limited for large securities markets, they are more relevant for thinner traded securities and assets. We can then concentrate on the price impact costs related to the bid-ask spread: these will vary according to the size of the transactions and will be limited for small positions but can increase with larger positions, thus affecting the bid-ask spread if the size is significantly larger than the standard market-makers' quoted size.

We can then proceed with the calculation of liquidity risk, this being the increase in costs ($L(q)$) changing through time, market conditions and frequency and sizes of trades: some common approaches to compute these liquidity costs are briefly presented so as to provide some elements for a complete liquidity risk valuation. Further reading is listed in the bibliography and is beyond the scope of this text.

Banks are required to calculate a standard, daily, relative Value-at-Risk and we maintain this in the presented cases. A first simple liquidity adjustment of a VaR measure can be factored in using the bid-ask spread. One approach is to determine liquidity risk as the worst possible transaction price and therefore the worst bid-ask spread is added to the worst mid-price. The liquidity-adjusted total risk could then be computed as:

$$L - VaR = \exp(z\sigma_r) + (\mu_s + \hat{z}_s\sigma_s)$$

where σ_r represents the variance of the continuous mid-price return over the appropriate time horizon while μ_s and σ_s are respectively the mean and variance of the bid-ask spread. z is the percentile of the normal distribution for the given confidence, factor $\hat{z}_s$ is the empirical percentile of the spread distribution in order to account for non-normality in the bid-ask spreads. Applying this approach implies that bid-ask spreads can increase over time, which is particularly valid during crises, but does not take into account the fact that liquidity costs also augment with order size beyond quoted market-maker size, so it could underestimate the liquidity impact. Though pretty simple, this is a model that is easy to implement, relying on data that are mostly available.

An alternative way to account for liquidity in VaR modelling is considering future time variation of prices and spreads and rather than assuming a normal distribution for future prices and taking the historical distribution for future spreads, applying non-normal distributions for prices and spreads, in order to consider skewness and kurtosis. This alternative parametric specification defines relative, liquidity-adjusted total risk as:

$$L - VaR = 1 - \exp(\mu_r + \hat{z}_r\sigma_r) \times \left(1 - \frac{1}{2}(\mu_s + \hat{z}_s\sigma_s)\right)$$

where μ_r, μ_s and σ_r, σ_s are the mean and variance of the mid-price return and spread respectively. $\hat{z}_r$, $\hat{z}_s$ represent the non-normal distribution percentile adjusted for skewness and kurtosis, according to the Cornish–Fisher expansion:

$$\hat{z} = z + \frac{1}{6}(z^2 - 1) * \gamma + \frac{1}{24}(z^3 - 3z) * k - \frac{1}{36}(2z^3 - 5z) * \gamma^2$$

where z is the appropriate percentile of the normal distribution, γ is the skewness and k the excess kurtosis of the respective distribution. This approach yields more precise risk forecasts than the first approach described.

Another approach is to identify the liquidity price effect from a regression of past trades while controlling for other risk factors. From this point of view, future price is driven by risk factor changes and the liquidity impact of trading N_t number of securities as follows:

$$P_{mid,t+1} - P_{mid,t} = C + \theta N_t + x_{t+1} + \varepsilon_t$$

where θ is the regression coefficient, x is the effect of risk factor changes on the mid-price, C is a constant and ε_t the error term of the regression. θ can be explained as the absolute liquidity cost per security traded. Although based on transactional data, one can approximate the transaction price with $P_{mid,t+1}$, so the market risk effects are:

$$x_{t+1} = \beta \times r_{M,\,t} \times P_{mid,\,t}$$

where $\beta = \mathrm{Cov}(r, r_M)/\sigma_{r_{market}}$ is the beta factor for each individual security return on a set portfolio, with a value-weighted portfolio return r_M over a set period. This can vary significantly depending on standard deviation, minimum and maximum. The average liquidity costs per individual security are very small. One can calculate continuous, liquidity-adjusted net return as:

$$rnet_t(q) = \ln\left(1 + \left[\beta \times r_{M,t} - \theta \times \frac{N_t + n}{P_{mid,t}} \right] \right)$$

for each standard-volume number of security $n = q/P_{mid,\,t}$ to allow for later comparison with other liquidity risk models. We can assume the full position will be liquidated at once and then define relative, liquidity-adjusted total risk as:

$$L - VaR(q) = 1 - \exp\left(\mu_{rnet(q)} + z\sigma_{rnet(q)} \right)$$

where $\mu_{rnet(q)}$ is the 20-day rolling net return mean and $\sigma_{r_{net(q)}}$ is the estimated net return variance (EWMA). z is the empirical percentile of the net return distribution. While this liquidity measure seems to be quite noisy, the approach has the general advantage of being based on transaction data only and therefore it is a valid alternative in those markets where liquidity cost data are not available.

There are models that consider the fact that liquidity cost increases with order size by using limit order book data. Then one can use the liquidity cost measure weighted spread, which calculates the liquidity costs compared with the fair price when liquidating a position quantity q against the limit order book. Weighted spread WS can be calculated as follows:

$$WS_t(q) = \frac{a_t(v) - b_t(v)}{P_{mid,t}}$$

$\alpha_t(v)$ is the volume-weighted ask price of trading v shares calculated as $\alpha_t(v) = \sum_i a_{i,t} v_{i,t}/v$ with $a_{i,t}$ being the ask price and $v_{i,t}$ the ask volume of individual limit orders. An order of size q is executed against several limit orders until individual limit order sizes add up to q. The weighted spread is similar to the bid-ask spread and is the cost of a round-trip for position q.

Mid prices present the average values between bid and ask prices, and can be used for VaR calculation. This approach is not appropriate in reality, as the price of the transaction differs from the mid-price (note that the sale is implemented applying the bid price while the purchase will take the ask price). In addition, if the volume of the position exceeds the normal market size, then bid and ask prices move in an adverse direction to the one desired, so that if the trader is liquidating a large position then the bid price will be going down once the traded quantity exceeds the normal market size. Thus, the market liquidity risk can be divided into exogenous liquidity risk, associated with the observed bid-ask spread, and endogenous liquidity risk, connected to the influence of the liquidated quantity on the price of the asset. One way to deal with market liquidity risk is to set limits on positions in the portfolio, as it can enable the avoidance of sufficient losses when one wants to liquidate the position.

The market can be characterized as a deep market or thin market according to the level of impact of sales on price (if the influence of a traded quantity on price is not significant and the realized spread does not differ much from the observed one, then the market can be referred to as a deep market; if the effect on price is large enough, then the market is thin). As an example of deep markets, the markets of highly-liquid securities (such as treasury securities, main currencies) can be considered; the depth itself reflects the activity of participants in the market and volume of trading. Another two characteristics of liquidity of the market are tightness and resilience. Tightness shows how far the price of the transaction deviates from the mid-price, resilience reflects the time necessary for the price to return to its levels after the transaction is conducted. As in certain models that will be considered below, spread is used in order to account for the liquidity component in VaR; it will therefore be useful to look at the concept of spread in more detail.

Some researchers point out that spread reflects three types of costs: order processing costs (these costs are associated, for example, with the state of technology, cost of trading), asymmetric information costs (these refer to orders coming from informed traders) and inventory-carrying costs (present the costs of maintaining open positions). Models, associated with spread can be used for incorporating exogenous and endogenous liquidity risk in the VaR framework.

This research can be divided into two broad classes. First there are models that consider the problem of accounting for the endogenous liquidity risk by searching for optimal liquidation strategies of a position. This is important as immediate liquidation of a position results in high costs, but in the case of slow liquidation the position is exposed to price risk, so there is a trade-off between execution costs and price risk and the problem of finding the optimal trading strategy appears. The latter can be done by minimizing transaction cost or maximizing expected revenue from trading, then, based on the received optimal strategy, liquidity-adjusted value at risk can be derived. The second class of models is devoted to modelling exogenous liquidity risk through studying the distribution of spread. In addition, certain modifications allow the inclusion of endogenous liquidity risk in this class of models. But before we start with models presenting the approaches of the first group, we should mention the ad hoc method of adjustment.

4.3   VAR LIQUIDATION-ADJUSTED

One of the easiest ways of adding liquidity risk in VaR models is to adjust the time horizon of VaR according to the inherent liquidity of the portfolio. In spite of adjusting the time horizon to the inherent liquidity of the portfolio, the calculation of value at risk assumes that the liquidation of all positions is taken at the end of the holding period rather than taken in orderly fashion during the given period; if the liquidation of the portfolio is taken as orderly throughout the set horizon period, the liquidation-adjusted value at risk is then obtained. We begin with the model for one asset and one risk factor. The main idea is to calculate the mean and variance of the portfolio value defined when the liquidation is over, but the important point here is that the portfolio is liquidated by parts during the holding period. The initial position is assumed to be uniformly liquidated over the period T. The liquidation schedule is characterized by the sequence of trade dates and volumes executed. The logarithm of the ratio of the risk factor's levels is assumed to be normally distributed, portfolio value at time T can be computed as the sum of products of the sold number of units of asset and the price of sale. After certain transformations, the variance of portfolio value is obtained and on this basis the liquidation-adjusted value at risk can be found (it is computed as the usual value at risk, but due to the fact that liquidation is taken throughout the holding period, the variance differs from the ordinary case, thus the obtained value at risk also differs from standard VaR measures).

The difference between the two measures represents the liquidation factor and it depends on the number of trading dates. If the number of trading dates tends to infinity, then the liquidation factor approaches one third. We also extend this model to the case of a portfolio of multiple assets that are influenced by multiple risk factors. More complex derivations lead to the same result in the relation between liquidation-adjusted value at risk and the usual one. We then introduce exogenous and endogenous liquidity costs by constructing the liquidation price of the asset (endogenous liquidity cost presents the sensitivity of liquidation price to trade size). This liquidation price is used to calculate the portfolio value at time T, thus, liquidation-adjusted and liquidity-cost adjusted value at risk (LA-VaR) is obtained. The holding period can then be considered as an endogenous variable and found as an output of the model. The liquidation schedule defines the level of VaR and I propose that we consider the minimum of these values to be LA-VaR: for some given trading frequency the number of trading dates that minimizes the derived VaR can be calculated. The liquidation period T is computed as the product of trading frequency and the optimal number of trading dates.

In contrast to permanent market impact, temporary market impact exists only in the period when liquidation of the certain block of shares takes place: selling of n securities in the interval between $t-n$ and t influences the price only in this time interval and does not influence the price in consequent time intervals. In order that the temporary market impact disappears in the next period, the price of stock has to increase by the value of the temporary market impact in order that only the permanent market impact remains at the beginning of the next period. The temporary market impact function can also be assumed to be a linear function of the average rate of trading, having an additional term that represents fixed costs of selling.

There is the problem of finding the optimal execution strategy but in the case of an endogenous holding period with the assumption of sales at constant speed. A possibility is to assume permanent and temporary market impact functions are included in the model of price movement (however, the sales price at time k is determined by the deduction of the temporary market impact function from the price of that period). On the basis of a given model of price movement, transaction costs are found as the difference between the initial value of the position and the liquidation value. Then, mathematical expectation and variance of transaction costs can be derived. A function has to be minimized in order to obtain the optimal execution strategy, this being the sum of mathematical expectation of transaction costs and the product of multiplication of standard deviation of transaction costs, cost of capital *r* and a certain percentile of standard normal distribution, determined by the investor's risk aversion. While the first term of the sum presents the average change in the value of the position, the second term reflects the influence of market risk. Minimization of the described function under the condition of sales at constant speed with respect to the number of sales enables us to find the optimal number of sales and the optimal holding period. Then the liquidation-adjusted VaR can be defined as the relative VaR and equals the product of a percentile of standard normal distribution for a given confidence level and standard deviation of transaction costs which occur in the case of the optimal trading strategy.

Another possibility is to account for liquidity risk in the usual VaR framework considering the influence of the amount of sold assets on prices, and on the basis of these prices estimate portfolio value. The value of the portfolio is supposed to be determined by positions in assets and the pricing function which defines the effect of risk factors on the portfolio value. The changes in asset price are connected to those of the volume of the position in this asset. A negative slope observed can be explained on the basis of the theory of asymmetric information: selling large amounts of asset can be read as a signal and therefore the effect on asset valuation will be included in the price. The effect will be linear and the total impact will be a negative effect resulting as a set multiplier of the amount executed. The trader faces the problem of maximizing expected revenue from trading over the whole holding period subject to the condition that the sum of traded shares has to be equal to a given number of shares. The price of the following period equals the price of the previous period adjusted to the market-wide change in the price of the share and the term presenting the influence of the amount of sold shares on the price. The optimal number of trading securities is found from the maximization problem. Then, the solution is plugged into the equation which defines the process of price movement, and consequently the portfolio value can be obtained. The latter appears to consist of two terms: one is responsible for the market risk component and corresponds to the price of the previous period and the market-wide change in price, the other term reflects the reaction of the price on the amount of asset sold, the effect of influence of the liquidating position on the price. The mathematical expectation and variance of the portfolio value can be calculated (the market-wide change in price and number of shares sold are assumed to be independent, this leads to an additional term in the expression for variance). The parameter in the equation for price movement is obtained as the estimation from regression, where the dependent variable is the difference in prices between two periods. Thus, the calculation of value at risk is based on the rebuilding of portfolio values, which accounts for the decrease in price from optimal investor's sales.

The distribution of portfolio values can be estimated by numerical methods. It is possible to pay attention not only to the market impact of sales on the price of an asset, but also to the existence of execution lag, so that the sale is not executed immediately after the order arrives. These two points are considered as features of liquidity, the case of absence of execution lag and market impact is the case of absence of liquidity risk. If the price of stock follows geometric Brownian motion, the impact of sales on price is included with the help of a price discount function that has certain properties (one of the properties is that the function is non increasing in sales) and existence of the execution lag is defined by the sales function dynamics (the latter means that the larger the sale is, the more time it will take to execute this order). The aim of the trader, who has some number of shares, is to find such a strategy of liquidation that will maximize the expected revenue from the sale. If the trader is a price taker (the case of no liquidity risk), then the optimal trading strategy for him is block liquidation of assets. Depending on whether the drift in the price process is positive or negative, the block liquidation has to be taken, respectively, at a terminal date or immediately. In the case of liquidity risk, the optimal execution strategy will be the same as in the previous case only if the condition of economies of scale in trading holds. This condition provides that the cumulative price discount in the case of selling all shares in two parts is less than or equal to the price discount in the case of selling all the shares at once. The liquidity discount is computed then as the difference between the market price of the share and its liquidation value. The calculation of liquidity-adjusted value at risk, based on this model, requires knowledge of average and standard deviation of price discount for the number of shares sold and of the execution period.

These models deal with endogenous liquidity risk, however, it is not so easy to apply these methods in practice due to the limited data available and difficulties in determining some of the parameters of the models (for example, the coefficient of proportionality of the temporary market impact function).

One can make a strong distinction between exogenous liquidity risk, which is similar for all market participants and cannot be influenced by the actions of one player and presents the market characteristics, and the endogenous liquidity risk, which is special for each player according to the volume of trading position, as after the volume exceeds the level of quote depth, the traded size has an influence on bid and ask prices. The possibility of including the exogenous liquidity risk in the VaR model is that in the case of not perfectly liquid markets, the liquidation of the position is not executed at mid-price, as this price has to be adjusted for the value of the existing spread. Thus, because in order to compute the usual VaR the worst price of the asset for some confidence level is considered, then in order to account for the effect of spread on the price of transaction in the VaR calculation, the worst value of the spread for a certain confidence level has to be considered.

4.3.1 Exogenous and endogenous liquidity risk in the VaR model

Some extend such analysis to account for endogenous risk, substituting the bid-ask spread used for the value at risk calculation for the

Weighted Average Spread (WAS). WAS is connected to the market, where the sale and purchase of large blocks of assets are allowed to be performed in one transaction and its price has to be in the interval defined by WAS for a block of standard size. The WAS presents the difference between weighted bids and asks: bids and asks are weighted according to the quantities indicated in the buy- and sell-orders (orders are added up in order to reach a standard size of block) and these weighted sums are then divided by the quantity, corresponding to the block's standard size. Thus, transactions with a number of shares in the block equal to or greater than the standard size will be taken at some price from the described interval. This means that now the second term in the formula for LA-VaR also incorporates the influence of traded size on the price of stock, and accounts for endogenous risk. Empirical estimation of the part of LA-VaR related to liquidity risk changes in the case of incorporation of endogenous liquidity risk in comparison with the case when only exogenous risk was included in LA-VaR. The component responsible for liquidity risk has increased after calculations with WAS.

4.3.2 Liquidity risk horizons

The Basel Committee for Banking Supervision has recently issued a revised proposed framework to measure and control market risk, in fact the first thorough revision since the first accord was published some fifteen years ago. The new framework explicitly considers market risk calculation in the factoring of liquidity impact as banks could be hampered from closing the positions or hedging without a negative impact on market prices, an important element to be included in the VaR. In addition, large increases or changes in the compensation required by investors to hold illiquid instruments can produce substantial mark-to-market losses on fair-valued instruments as liquidity conditions deteriorate.

The new approach for factoring in market liquidity risk is through the incorporation of varying liquidity horizons in the market risk metric. This seeks to account for the fact that firms might be unable to promptly hedge or exit certain risk positions without materially affecting market prices. This is broadly in line with the direction taken under Basel 2.5, which introduced varying liquidity horizons as part of the Incremental Risk Charge and the Comprehensive Risk Measure.

A liquidity horizon is defined as the time required to execute transactions that extinguish an exposure to a risk factor, without moving the price of the hedging instruments, in stressed market conditions. This implies that liquidity horizons will be assigned to risk factors rather than to instruments. This is in recognition of the fact that some risk factors driving the valuation of a financial instrument might be easier to hedge than others in periods of financial market stress.

In the new proposal the risk factors will be assigned to five generic liquidity horizon categories, ranging from a minimum of 10 days to one year. The shortest liquidity horizon, being the most liquid one, is in line with the current 10-day VaR treatment in the trading book. The longest liquidity and least liquid horizon matches the banking book horizon at one year. This will deliver a more graduated treatment of risks across the balance sheet and should also serve to reduce arbitrage opportunities between the banking and trading books.

In making this framework operational, a regulatory grouping of risk factors into broad categories has been devised, each of which is associated with one of five liquidity horizons. Risk factors are grouped into separate categories; the definition of the buckets is relatively broad, entailing some risk sensitivity costs. From an operational perspective, the banks will be required to map their own risk factors to this regulatory grouping and assign the relevant liquidity horizon for the purposes of market risk modelling. Each of the main risk types, namely interest rate risk, credit risk, foreign exchange risk and equities and commodities risk, is included. This is meant to capture all risk factors that would not fall under any of the other buckets.

A key operational consideration in the context of incorporating varying liquidity horizons in the regulatory market risk metric is how to apply risk factor shocks over longer and varying horizons. It is recognized that for firms using historical simulation modelling techniques, non-overlapping returns would be impracticable in the case of risk factors with relatively long liquidity horizons. For example, a sample of 100 returns would require more than eight years of historical data if the liquidity horizon were set at one month; it has been agreed that overlapping returns could be used to tackle this issue.

The varying liquidity horizons will be incorporated in the market risk metric under the assumption that banks are able to shed their risk at the end of the liquidity horizon. Accordingly, a liquidity horizon of three months would mean that the calculation of the regulatory capital charge would assume that the bank could hedge or exit its risk positions after three months and not require any rebalancing assumptions. This differs from the current requirements under the IRC, which require banks to calculate capital using a constant level of risk over a one-year capital horizon. This proposed liquidation approach recognizes the dynamic nature of banks' trading portfolios but, at the same time, it also recognizes that not all risks can be unwound over a short time period, which was a major flaw of the 1996 framework.

Market liquidity is a dynamic concept and, as such, it is to be expected that it will periodically revisit its assignment of liquidity horizons to reflect changes in market structures.

4.4 CASH FLOWS AT RISK

We have presented in brief in the previous section liquidity-adjusted VaR model literature, a wide area of research and analysis that looks at embedding the different degree of securities liquidity into their pricing and risk measurement.

Here we present a different aspect of liquidity risk, cash flow at risk, intended as the possibility that projected cash flows and securities' value available to refinance the bank's liquidity needs will vary and the result will be different from that expected. This can be defined as cash flows at risk and starts from the cash flow static ladder (see Chapter 2), introducing elements of probability to it.

General cash flow at risk modelling considers the inflows and outflows, as in the maturity ladder. These are divided into flows that do not have elements of uncertainty and therefore are static. Then there are flows that are not precisely predictable, as discussed previously, making here a distinction between the stressed hypothesis and actual ex-post cash inflow/outflow volatility intended as the difference between ladder ex-ante posting flows and registered ones.

Determining Cash Flow at Risk requires first cash flow modelling, distinguishing flows that vary according to market parameters (CF_v), unexpected cash flows (related to structural changes in the businesses, like disposing of certain activities) (CF_u), stable flows (CF_s) and flows adjusted for prediction errors (CF_e), so that the total flows to calculate LaR are:

$$CF_t = \sum_i CF_{v,i} + CF_{u,i} + CF_{s,i} + CF_{e,i}$$

Cash flow at risk can then be calculated from historical or simulated times series of CF_t, at a certain confidence level (q), assuming for example that the cash flow is normally distributed. Such assumptions will need statistical testing verification.

CHAPTER 5

Control Framework

This chapter looks at the processes banks should set forth in controlling funding liquidity risks and it summarizes the analysis so far. The Basel Committee issued some guidance principles on liquidity that are discussed in the first section. The second section looks into the specific control processes for liquidity that banks are expected to develop or have in place, taking into account lessons learnt from the recent crisis. The third section more specifically looks at monitoring and reporting, an increasingly relevant element for auditors and regulators. The fourth section presents options and indications for liquidity risk limit setting and the fifth the contingency liquidity plan process, this also being an important element of the control framework.

5.1 GOVERNANCE PRINCIPLES

The Basel Committee for Banking Supervision published a list of sound practice principles for banks' adequate liquidity management. These are a set of guidance rules for banks to apply in liquidity risk management and control, rather than being compulsory rules, the principles outline the behaviours and process shape one should have in assessing and managing liquidity risk. One can find many aspects and principles in common with other risk types and the same prudential approach is applied, aiming at greater managerial awareness and involvement in regular risk assessment.

There are many relevant elements and valid indications in these principles and it is worth going through some; these are indeed good rules for risk management that we should consider and strive to follow and are valuable for liquidity too. In this section the principles are presented and most are commented upon (for the full list, see the bibliography).

One principle introduces the concept of sound management of liquidity risk, namely that a bank should establish a robust liquidity risk management framework that ensures it maintains sufficient liquidity, including a cushion of unencumbered, high quality liquid assets, to withstand a range of stress events, including those involving the loss or impairment of both unsecured and secured funding sources (abstract from Basel 3 capital accord). As presented and discussed at length, these are the pillars of a bank's liquidity, the LCR with counterbalancing capacity, the stress testing analysis to ascertain the impact of drained funding sources and the capacity on the one side to replace such sources and on the other – specifically for regulators – the potential impact of an individual bank's failure to the entire financial system. These principles are meant to support banks' management and banking regulators in defining and implementing a reliable and strong liquidity management and control framework, capable of withstanding crisis and evolving, learning from mistakes and promptly addressing weaknesses.

One of the governance principles introduces the concept of liquidity risk tolerance, indicating banks should assess and set liquidity risk appetite and then articulate the liquidity risk management and control accordingly. As part of a review process started with the Basel 2 framework and then resulting in the Internal Capital Adequacy Assessment Process, banks' senior management and risk control functions are to quantify and set the liquidity internal risk limits and coherent capital. Articulated from the total onto the various types of risk exposures, we shall include liquidity risk in the types we need to encompass in the ICAAP framework.

Once the liquidity risk appetite is set, rules and a process for its management and control shall be defined accordingly and consistently. This principle, as for other risk types, assumes we set forth internal rules for liquidity risk that need to be assessed and approved by the company's board of directors. Such rules describe the framework and support both the strategic and operational liquidity risk management: such rules will be updated regularly and whenever it becomes necessary (e.g. changing organization or legal requirements). Though the sound practice principles provide just generic indications on how policies and strategies should be articulated, banks are expected to interpret and articulate it so as to ensure an operational indication and clear rules for strategic and contingency liquidity management. The following are some hints based on experience in internal policy drafting: (1) it is pretty important to differentiate the parts or sections that need constant annual updating from those that are more likely to remain unchanged for longer; (2) list the core goals or targets to be achieved by such policies; (3) be cautious when listing systems and specific procedures, as these might change and could still be work in progress.

Pricing of liquidity is another cornerstone explicitly indicated in a dedicated sound practice principle. We are expected to include or take clearly into account liquidity costs, the benefits and risk exposure in the internal pricing modes/rules, the staff performance assessment and the new product assessment process. This should be done for all relevant activities that are somehow exposed to liquidity risk or could impact liquidity exposure. We shall look at the consistency between staff reward incentives and the impact on the bank's liquidity exposures, making sure that this does not lead to or potentially cause an unwanted or greater liquidity risk. An element of great relevance both for regulatory and reputational reasons is setting internal rules and methods to quantify the liquidity cost associated with individual transactions and disclosing such cost to external and internal customers (business lines, functions). The performance and incentive remuneration systems should be taking such cost clearly into account: this will be a key component of the bank's liquidity management framework. This aspect of liquidity management hasn't been much addressed in previous chapters: the cost of liquidity and its allocation constitutes a very important element. Given all the matter linked to products or services, pricing is a very sensitive issue, we need adequate measuring systems and available data. Reaching an internal agreement on allocation across the different functions and business involved isn't often a simple process, especially when it is based on estimates or model gauging analysis. On the one side it is important that the customers/functions realize and accept that liquidity has a cost, and the bank itself ultimately bears it, on the other side the mechanism deriving from any allocation ought to be consistent with the set risk appetite and the behaviours expected.

A different and specific principle on liquidity quantification and control is the one requiring that the *bank should have a sound process for identifying, measuring, monitoring and controlling liquidity risk*. As discussed at length in previous chapters, the measurement framework should span cash flows, available funding sources and securities stocks capacity.

A recurrent constraint for banking groups is the actual possibility of transferring funds between legal entities, often assuming this is promptly available when needed. We need to be aware and regularly monitor the *risk exposures and funding needs within and across legal entities, business lines and currencies, taking into account legal, regulatory and operational limitations to the transferability of liquidity*. This is an assessment that ought to be backed by a legal and regulatory analysis that is foremost necessary to ensure that liquidity can be transferred. We might find it hard and complex and often some assumptions are laid out, but using some simple rules for this assessment can prove an acceptable proxy (for example, set percentage of the equity capital).

The funding risk, intended here as the diversification of financing sources and counterparties, is another relevant element that is specifically listed by another sound practice principle. We must assess and strive to ensure the company keeps diversified and balanced sources of funding; it is also necessary to guarantee a solid presence in the money markets. The bank's reputation and perceived solidity is of paramount importance, especially in times of financial stress: a negative press and news may ultimately affect its funding sources and can hamper liquidity capacity.

Intraday liquidity risk is increasingly a monitoring necessity, as amply discussed in Chapter 2. It is important that we outline internal processes and rules to monitor intraday liquidity risk and specific indicators and warning levels. It is important to have it as part of the risk appetite framework and it should be part of regular monitoring mechanisms.

Further principles cover collateral posting, stress testing and contingency management. The increased attention paid to collateral posting, its quality and valuation, has a major role in counterparty credit risk assessment and likewise for liquidity risk management. The bank's treasury and risk control function are responsible for managing and monitoring collateral posting: trends, securities value and credit quality, both at closing and intraday, including the possibility of its intercompany and cross-country analysis transferability, should be analysed.

As addressed at length, stress testing valuations are another fundamental liquidity analysis to be performed: the bank should carry out stress tests on a regular basis encompassing several types of parameters and the results and indications derived from such analysis should also be included in liquidity management and control, both for the end of day and intraday processes.

Linked to the stress testing analysis is the contingency funding plan and related processes. The structure of such a plan should consider concrete actions to be taken and listed in the annual contingency plan update, that must be formally presented to the senior management committees and the board. The bank's funding liquidity counterbalancing capacity (see previous chapters) is meant to provide a cushion of unencumbered, high quality liquid assets to be held as insurance against a range of liquidity stress scenarios, including those that involve the loss or impairment of unsecured and normally accessible funding sources. It is expected that this will also be an integral part of the bank's liquidity contingency plan assessment.

5.2 CONTROL PROCESSES

We will now discuss and focus on the liquidity risk management control process that firms should have in order to control and react properly – and promptly – to a liquidity crisis. Banks should define the different forms of liquidity risk to which they are exposed (including relevant subsets within each form defined); identify where they fit in their enterprise risk universe; and communicate these definitions across their groups so that a common understanding is applied when identifying and evaluating liquidity risk related to existing businesses, business reviews, new businesses, products or initiatives, and acquisitions and alliances.

We distinguish between funding liquidity risk and market liquidity risk. Within funding liquidity risk, we should look at control processes for the contingency and structural long-term period, the shorter term and the intraday. The risk control processes should provide accurate and detailed references on the governance mechanism (relevant information, delegation of powers, escalation), a set of rules for risk quantification, including scenario analysis, regular monitoring and contingency planning. These control processes will need to be maintained and be up to date, reflecting organizational or regulatory changes. Liquidity risk functions should regularly update the control process and the documentation.

The company's liquidity documentary framework should encompass both strategies and policies. The strategies should indicate the specific risk appetite in terms of liquidity risk and its portfolio and funding set-up, firstly for the coming year and then longer term as well: as the equilibrium between long- and short-term funding determines the company's liquidity risk, we should have such an analysis as a core part of the annual liquidity strategy.

Policies are intended as guidelines on liquidity management and control standards that apply throughout the organization. They serve as a reference rule set, and as such we need these to be valid and functioning for longer cycles and supporting periods of market uncertainty. The company's board of directors should review and approve the liquidity strategy and preferably the relevant policies, as it is the board that is ultimately responsible for a company's adequate risk management systems and therefore needs a clear understanding of funding liquidity risks. We also need to update the board whenever there are relevant changes in the liquidity exposure, its measurement systems or regulatory requirements, in addition to regular updates on liquidity risks. It is also the board's responsibility to ensure that the company's management sets and updates internal liquidity risk management and control processes – organizational structures to ensure approved strategies and policies can be applied.

While aware that liquidity risk management remains a cost and liquidity management can also generate a conflict of interest if we try to exploit it for profit generation rather than ensuring best management, we need to indicate and separate within the company the profit from the service centres: the company's liquidity management ensures best interests if its goals are not profit related but rather the long-term balance of funding and lending and maintaining a sound asset buffer in cases of market stress. We need to correctly identify and allocate liquidity costs to the different business lines, so that it is correctly within the performance measurement and risk incentives. Another potential conflict of interest related to liquidity is the role played by the market functions and the treasury functions, the latter being the one that manages the overall liquidity of the company and disposes of the deposits and collateral. It is therefore key that we define an internal model or rule – as part of the liquidity strategy and rules set – ensuring there are transparent and valid incentive mechanisms in place: liquidity is vital for the long-term survival of the company and incentives must be designed to guarantee long-term balance is preserved. Such mechanisms should also be extended to off-balance-sheet products. In the strategic part of liquidity risk management, we should measure the different liquidity related costs and have a price related to liquidity risk for the different instruments/exposures. We also need an allocation mechanism for such costs so that conflicts of interest and dangerous incentives are addressed: the treasury's function is best kept as a non-profit centre, while profit-generating functions should have a short-term as well as long-term liquidity cost charge.

5.2.1 Functions in charge of liquidity risk management and control

There are no specific regulatory indications in terms of organizational set-up for the liquidity risk management and control functions. Basic requirements applying to all risk management are also valid for liquidity. Here we should take into account the fact that the first level responsibility for the liquidity balance needs to be correctly positioned in the organization so that its primary goal is to ensure funding is never at risk and the overall assets and liabilities are matched. Whether we have a liquidity risk management function with revenues setting primary goals could affect the liquidity risk profile and expose the company to funding risks. When designing and reviewing the organizational structure we should make sure there is independent managerial formal hierarchical reporting for risk-taking functions and the functions responsible for monitoring. Both regulators and empirical evidence therefore suggest maintaining it as a neutral service approach function, without profit targets, but rather with quality service or targets linked to liquidity ratios and funding equilibrium. A further element to consider is the appropriate level of power delegation in the funding liquidity responsibility assigned to the company's functions, in particular when it comes to an overall group responsibility and individual legal entity control: we need to carefully design the organization so that the overall liquidity management and control is assigned to dedicated functions, whose responsibility must also include the individual legal entity liquidity risk, with a defined steering role over all the controlled legal entities that are exposed to funding liquidity risks. In many companies, the liquidity risk control activities, such as policies and procedures drafting, risk measurement and monitoring, are centralized, while the day-to-day liquidity risk control is more frequently decentralized, especially for large, international banks.

5.2.2 Risk committees

It is common to give liquidity risk oversight responsibility to dedicated committees: in many cases these are asset and liability committees or risk committees. The powers and control roles formally assigned to such committees and the representing members are very important; we should pay attention to the following:

- There must be a committee that is the first and ultimate body in charge of the liquidity risk of the company and for the group.
- Members must include all the relevant functions that are in charge of the various elements determining liquidity exposures.
- Formal powers must be consistent with management and supervisory roles on liquidity.
- Overlap with other committees should also be assessed and verified to avoid inconsistency.
- Liquidity exposures and analysis must be timely and regularly presented to this committee, including individual legal entities and the overall group.

- Liquidity exposures in the intraday, short term and balance sheet structure must all be presented and included in the formal committee's responsibilities.

The possibility of a dedicated Liquidity Risk Committee might also be a valid one, ensuring the key points listed above apply. Experience suggests that it is preferable to rely on a limited set of management committees and that it is also preferable to include liquidity as part of one of the main risk committees in order to receive the correct focus from senior management, and also to combine it with other risk assessment, as often liquidity exposures are affected by market conditions.

5.2.3 Coordinating liquidity management

The rationale for centralizing and having one company dealing with the market for the whole group is the cost advantages of having one entry point and interface to the financial markets. In addition, centralizing the liquidity management also provides for optimization within the legal entities in the same group, as it allows for compensating opposing liquidity requirements within a financial group, from a company that might experience surplus to an entity that requires funding. There can be business cases where some companies are structurally in liquidity excess or structurally in funding need, a centralized liquidity management will support and optimize such imbalances. One element to keep under control is the legal and regulatory requirements that might hamper fund transfer within the same group of companies.

Another important element in favour of centralized liquidity management is a contingency set-up that might encounter regulatory approval: contingency funding in the case of market difficulties could be arranged to cross legal entities belonging to the same group. In stressed conditions, if there are carefully validated legal rules in place, we might shift liquidity from one legal entity to another in the same group, potentially also across countries, avoiding market funding constraints and costs. For this to be feasible, legal entities must be able and authorized to transfer funds to companies in the group. Centralizing liquidity management might be severed due to formal or political constraints on liquidity flows: we must map and assess these and monitor the actual funds available for contingency intragroup funding. Such constraints may be operational, for example access to common settlement systems, or curbed by internal credit limits, legal or regulatory constraints.

5.2.4 Liquidity risk monitoring function

We need to have a dedicated function in charge of funding liquidity risk control, independent from both the business functions and that responsible for the liquidity management. It is quite common in companies that such a liquidity risk control function is part of the risk control area, typically in charge of all the different risk types – market, operational, credit, counterparty – as liquidity risk is indeed very much related to other risk types that can also trigger liquidity exposures (see collateral management, asset prices available for refinancing, operational and reputational risks in terms of market perception of a company's credit standing). The liquidity risk oversight function should then be articulated to ensure a presence in the controlled legal entities where there is a relevant liquidity management need and exposure, at the same time providing for group-wide coordination and oversight. As indicated earlier, coordination and oversight are necessary for regulatory and managerial purposes, to ensure limit compliance and rebalancing within the same group of companies. Such a set-up must be supported by articulated governance and monitoring rules. In addition, common reporting, limit sets and information technology systems strengthen such coordination.

5.2.5 Addressing documentation-related liquidity risks

Liquidity risk can also derive from transactions' contractual obligations, the collateral requirements (e.g. CSA standards, early termination clauses), securitization-related optionality and special liquidity requirements in the case of credit downgrades or other events triggering additional asset posting. The liquidity monitoring process should encompass these types of assets and exposures, including stress testing analysis to ascertain additional requirements. Liquidity exposure monitoring should involve the receipt of regular information on such clauses and any relevant changes to covenants, in particular for large, structural, long-term and complex transactions. Likewise for collateral requirements and posting, the contractual elements in a trading arrangement, especially for over-the-counter derivatives between financial counterparties rather than through an exchange, require adequate systems to permit a daily liquidity assessment and reciprocal posting of collateral requirements on large derivative portfolios, combined with repos and tri-party repos; this is of fundamental importance for appropriate representation and quantification of the liquidity exposure and possible requirements. Stress testing analysis is necessary to ascertain possible net outflows and unexpected liquidity claims, through varying time horizons: as collateral – cash or bonds or equities or other liquid securities – is a source of funding, the contractual types and termination clauses or replacement features need to be included in the scenario assessment.

Summarizing, the relevance of collateral in liquidity risk control is in the form of trades, especially derivatives and intraday netting and a bank's collateral management complexity needs to be appropriately taken into account for sound liquidity control. In order to master that complexity, we need to rely on a set of specific information, as listed below.

- *Cash flow dynamics*: we need a comprehensive set of data on collateral contractual inflows/outflows, and this needs to be updated daily.
- *Collateral posting:* where we have to know collateral needs precisely at adequate time intervals, considering current positions and possible future changes/evolution of portfolios as well as scenarios.
- *Stock available for posting:* we ought to know the required collateral amounts, and the types accepted by the different counterparties for various transaction types.
- *Monitoring of legal and operational constraints in place:* understanding and monitoring the various contracts binding the transactions in place in terms of required documentation, legal and operational issues is paramount in collateral and liquidity risk management. Indeed, this is probably the most complex issue to keep under control and render in the risk system databases.

In summary, collateral management should aim at optimizing the allocation of collateral available for different needs, across controlled legal entities and product types, ensuring a standard control. We need to measure the associated cost and in particular determine a specific liquidity charge by transaction type and collateral posted. We need detailed internal rules for collateral management and its control. For the latter, regular reporting needs should include the daily amounts of collateral, by asset and transaction type and by individual counterparty, with contractual clauses and maturity scheduled.

5.3 MONITORING LIQUIDITY EXPOSURE

Monitoring liquidity risk translates into regular reporting for the different elements that drive it and can influence exposure. We need to consider that reporting isn't simply a representation exercise, it is a core regulatory and managerial necessity; preparing and regularly producing reports is therefore a fundamental requirement and shouldn't be considered an administrative task and underestimated. In this section we'll look at the different regulatory reporting requirements, assessing the complexity of implementation. Whether those listed are the sole and best reporting data set will very much depend on available data, the market conditions in which the company mainly operates, the driving business lines and the risk management experience in controlling liquidity.

5.3.1 Available assets for refinancing

We need to set up daily and intraday reporting on immediate resources available for refinancing. This monitoring should be performed both by the function in charge of liquidity management and the function responsible for independent monitoring. Reporting of liquidity needs available should consider the assets under repo pledge and the prudential haircuts applicable. Information to senior management should also include stress testing additional analysis, thus also providing indications for deteriorating market conditions. It is also necessary to consider an adequate, prudential valuation of close out costs and the concentration of positions for such available assets, so that a fair valuation is computed and takes into account the bid-ask spreads and other market conditions in the valuation of reserves. We also need to keep under control both the customer collateral received that can be reused and the collateral reused maturing contractual schedule, with separate and dedicated monitoring. Reporting and regular monitoring is important and also includes the central bank facilities for the different asset classes available, presenting the facilities in place, utilization, the costs related and the haircuts applied. For a group operating in several countries, the central bank analysis will need to be extended to each country where such resources are available.

The monitoring needs to be carried out in the main reporting currency but we should have a separate analysis for all relevant currencies. Indeed the reporting of assets available for refinancing should consider the various liquidity needs for all the main currencies where we have operations and contractual obligations. Such monitoring is of paramount importance as often unexpected refinancing arises that went unnoticed in currencies where availability is limited (for either market or structural conditions) and the associated cost might be very high. Reporting on asset availability can be further enhanced and of managerial validity if combined with the maturity schedule of the various contractual obligations, in the different controlled legal entities and currencies (see the chapters on LCR and NSFR).

5.3.2 Funding concentration

As part of the core, standard regular monitoring of liquidity exposure, we need information on funding sources and concentration (see Chapter 2). We ought to verify that we are solely relying on limited and concentrated funding sources. Particular attention should also be paid to the breakdown control of concentration by currencies and by funding maturity. As part of the aggregate monitoring on liquidity funding sources concentration, it is also valuable to include information on the main controlled legal entities' individual positions, focusing on dependency from holding or central funding.

5.3.3 Liquidity coverage ratio and NSFR in the various currencies

Regulatory LCR and NSFR standards must be ensured in the main reporting currency; still, it is important to ensure monitoring of the LCRs and NSFRs in the core currencies and in the relevant legal entities. The consolidation exercise needs to be decoupled when it comes to monitoring both, as supervisors may be required to comply with minimum standards in relevant legal entities and because imbalances in one currency might affect the overall ratios' compliance.

5.3.4 Market-related monitoring tools

We introduced and discussed the liquidity indicators earlier in the book; supervisors also specifically require that some forward-looking monitoring is in place. Those set out and discussed hereafter are intended to anticipate as much as possible future liquidity crises or financial market deterioration:

- Market-wide information.
- Information on the financial sector.
- Company-specific information.

The combined monitoring of these indicators and information should support liquidity management and possibly allow for some anticipation of future market difficulties.

5.3.5 Overall market information

Regulators are asking banks to combine liquidity-specific information with that on the general condition of financial markets. There is no list of indicators to be considered here, suggestions are to include equity prices such as the country's overall stock markets and sector indices, debt markets and mainly money market levels, medium-term notes, long-term debts, derivative prices, government bond markets and credit default spread indices; foreign exchange markets for core currencies, commodities markets like oil or gold and indices related to specific products, such as for certain asset-backed securities. Such information is regularly monitored within a bank in managerial reporting and other various analyses. The recommendation is to have a tailored selection of variables that are

TABLE 5.1   Market-wide information.

Type	Liquidity forecasting power
Equity major index	limited predicting signals
Commodity prices	limited forecasting power, valuable in crisis
Banking equity sector	limited but higher than generic
Bond indexes	medium, more related to liquidity
Swap yield curves	medium–high, reflecting expectations
FX rates spot & forward	medium–high, varying market expectations

Source: The author.

particularly relevant for liquidity risk and longer term funding conditions. Those that might be additional valuable elements are listed in Table 5.1.

5.3.6   Information on the financial sector

Liquidity conditions and risk are very much linked to financial sector performance (banks, insurance, investment funds) and are surely more powerful for forecasting and monitoring information. We can use equity-specific indexes or other selective information from the credit rating to credit spread changes. Analysing the debt markets, in particular assessing the conditions of financial market access by banks and corporates, is of key importance, as well as monitoring the currencies, maturities and sizes of issuances. An important element will be the unsecured or non-asset-backed market access, as it has proved to be the first affected by liquidity risk. Credit spread over the highest rating curves is another important element to verify, as well as the funding capacity in different currencies. This might prove a very useful indicator of what we can measure as the market liquidity risk appetite, meaning the interest in acquiring securities issued by lower credit financial institutions and the spread paid in such placements.

5.3.7 Company-specific information

Liquidity management and control functions need to monitor the stability of their own organization, the elements of credit rating and spreads in the markets as well as the financial results and consensus on equity prices: if the market perceives weakness or has identified risks in the company then this will have an immediate impact on liquidity cost and funding capacity. Other banks will indeed likely reduce credit lines, investment and pension funds will be less likely to underwrite new securities issued, credit spreads and funding costs will jump: it might then be meaningful to monitor credit spreads, money-market levels and longer term funding conditions. Financial results must also be regularly combined with the information, in particular data on credit coverage and quality measurements.

5.3.8 Recommendations on the monitoring process

We've stressed the importance of providing boards, committees, liquidity management and control functions with regular – daily, quarterly, intraday – information sets on liquidity conditions or other possible indicators of financial market stability, combined with own company soundness and risk exposures. We need to pay even greater attention to the appropriate, professional and experienced interpretation and use of such numbers. Likewise for limit setting and breaches, the management and control functions must correctly interpret the changes in conditions and the relevance of various indicators, as some will be more critical and require intervention.

5.3.9 Reporting frequency and distribution

Regulators and sound practice principles indicate that reporting should reflect the company and organization set-up and be promptly changed. The reporting should be ensured throughout the year through a daily, monthly and quarterly update – also intraday for the relevant payments and collateral netting. Regulators expect that the LCR should report at least monthly, with the operational capacity to increase frequency to weekly or even daily in stressed situations, while the NSFR should be calculated and reported at least quarterly, with a contained time lag that should remain within 15 days for the LCR or the NSFR. For these, regulatory reporting applies on a consolidated basis; as indicated before, we may well have it for the relevant controlled legal entities or consistently within the organizational set-up.

5.4 SETTING LIQUIDITY RISK LIMITS

Liquidity risk, be it credit or market and operational, affects the desire and willingness of a firm to tolerate losses. Liquidity is a risk that can be thought of as binary, being more likely to lead to a bank's liquidation or default than mere losses, even huge ones. So one can imagine that limits and risk appetite setting for liquidity funding risk differ from those for credit or market risk in the fact that the ultimate result of missing payments is the firm defaulting. In setting limits, then, one must make sure that the risk tolerance here is survival of the organization.

Limits are prescribed by regulators and are therefore core statutory requirements. They are also necessary for risk appetite and risk-adjusted return. We can also distinguish between different limit types:

- Regulatory limits on liquidity coverage ratio and net stable funding ratio (see Chapters 3 and 4).
- Main managerial limits, either operational ones and/or linked to the institution's own risk appetite.
- Operational limits, for the restricted part of the organization or individual activities.

▪ Warning levels, monitoring measures activating pre-assessment mechanisms or analysis.

The 100% minima for LCR and NSFR were presented and discussed earlier in the book, banks should then assess and understand the cascade and individual unit or sub entity limits, whether these also should comply with the limits or whether the consolidated limits will be binding. Likewise, timeframes for individual business lines or legal entities must be set to appropriate levels and presented and justified to the board and regulators.

Managerial limits can differ in terms of levels and most can take different forms; in short, there could be a full set of completely different ratios that the risk committee and board are looking to assign, in addition to the regulatory ones.

Often, rather than formal limit sets, banks prefer warning levels, as these allow a more flexible discussion and prevent excessive reactions to hedge and intervene in order to comply with the limits set. Warning levels may prove useful or preferable for subsets or currencies or business units where a managerial action needs gauging.

5.4.1 Limit setting and review

The limits for liquidity risk are set to span the overall risk at bank or group level, and limits will be set for the individual legal entities controlled that are similar to the ones identified at the overall level. Limits should be envisaged for countries too. Then, further breakdown at business-line level will require an assessment of practical meaning and action that could be possibly undertaken. Here, the possibility of granular breakdowns and articulation must be a meaningful valuation of possible action to be taken. An annual review, together with ICAAP and risk tolerance process updates, should also include liquidity risk limits. Policies, internal procedures and communication should follow. The utilization level experienced, the business and the interested entities' feedback all need to be considered, a limit framework being a gauge in time rather than an absolute meter.

5.4.2 Reporting and escalation procedures

We need to distinguish an escalation process when different types of liquidity limits or warning levels are breached. It is important to ensure consistency between limits or warning relevance and the escalation procedure: we should not apply the same level of attention to breaches that have a substantially different impact on the company's liquidity exposure. The rules of thumb for escalation that we recommend are:

- Core limit breaches should be brought to the attention of and approved by the highest level risk committee (e.g. main currency short-term liquidity limit breaches).
- Lower, operational limits and warning levels are best managed without the committees' involvement.
- Multiple operational limit breaches should be presented to the relevant risk committee.
- Enduring over-limit exposures, even at operational limit level, must be addressed and presented to the risk committee for resolution.
- The warning level should have a dedicated escalation process in place.

On a regular basis a liquidity limits map, including warning levels, should be updated and presented to the relevant committee. The limit map should have all the limits in place, in each controlled legal entity and for each time horizon and currency.

Statistics on limits and warning level utilization and numbers of breaches are a helpful and recommended set of information for risk committees and the board. The liquidity risk control function should present such reporting at least quarterly and discuss the map and limit set alongside the risk appetite and budget review yearly.

5.4.3   Internal rules on limit setting and management

It is required and also necessary that we articulate the limit setting, review and breach management in an official company document. This will serve as a reference rule set. It should be the risk control function's responsibility to issue and update it, presenting it also to a relevant committee for validation.

5.5   CONTINGENCY LIQUIDITY PLAN

We have mentioned many times before the importance of contingency funding plans, these are essential in ensuring that emergency actions are outlined and should be different, in the procedures and the proposed actions, to routine liquidity management. We can ideally divide the contingency plans into market and balance sheet intervention and internal emergency procedures (we can refer to these as internal policies). We look at both here, however the market levers, as presented in the liquidity buffer chapter, are greatly driven by the risk tolerance and profitability targets of the bank, where higher quality securities, usually less remunerative, or cash are hoarded to face liquidity crises. The total amount and quality of these will result in a trade-off between the contingency safety net and revenues. Additionally, in addressing the level of security buffer, an important element to consider is the link between stress testing and contingency funding planning. Triggering events for contingency plans should be aligned to stress testing results. Conversely, experience from stress tests can be incorporated in contingency guidelines.

We can define a **contingency funding plan (CFP)** as a set of internal procedures for managing cash flow shortfalls in emergency situations. It incorporates assumptions about liquidity values of assets and buffers and the behaviour of liabilities, clients and regulators. The contingency plan encompasses a set of policies, procedures and action plans for managing liquidity stress events. The objectives of such a plan are to provide prompt and articulated instructions for responding to a liquidity crisis, to identify alternative liquidity sources that a covered company can access during liquidity stress events, and to describe steps that should be taken to ensure that the covered company's sources of liquidity are sufficient to fund its operating costs and meet its commitments while minimizing additional costs and disruption.

Although contingency plans are a more recent stringent regulatory requirement, many large banking groups have one established and rely on several years' experience. However, there appears to be a wide range of practices, from relatively simple operational procedures that set out the responsibilities of and reporting lines to the crisis management committee. The plans are designed to make it possible to make decisions rapidly and buy time in which to identify and think through the range of possible actions. Communication with markets and the public is essential, especially in name-specific events.

A contingency plan involves striking a balance between the need to have pre-existing procedures in order to be prepared when a crisis occurs, and the need for flexibility as the crisis develops. The contingency plan is usually formulated at the group level, and is supplemented by local ones. It is usually tailored to circumstances that can affect the individual liquidity position, such as idiosyncratic shocks or market disruptions.

While contingency actions can be tailored and be contingent scenario-specific, they typically share some objectives, namely reducing cash-consuming activities or maintaining franchise value, signalling to the market that the institution is in a financially good and stable condition.

Guidelines and industry standards indicate some common elements of a contingency plan:

- A list and description of the events triggering the plan.
- A list of the potential sources of funding on both the asset and liability sides (e.g. slowing loan growth, sale or repo of liquid assets, securitization, subsidiary sales, increasing deposit

growth, lengthening the maturities of liabilities as they mature, draw-down of committed facilities, raising capital and stopping dividends to parents).

- An escalation procedure detailing how additional funds can be identified and then provided.
- A procedure for the smooth management of the contingency, which should include a description of the delineation of responsibilities (including the responsibilities of the management body) and a process for ensuring timely information flows (for example, through contact lists).
- A procedure governing contacts with external parties, such as important counterparties, auditors, market analysts, press and media, and regulatory authorities.

It is of paramount importance for banks to perform regular testing of their contingency funding plans – and in particular the sources of funding listed in the plans – not only to prevent operational difficulties in times of crisis when the need to activate those sources arises, but also to reduce reputation risk and avoid sending the wrong signals to the market if those contingent sources are to be activated only in times of stress.

The contingency plan's adequacy must somehow be tested to make sure it indeed provides some safety nets. Its adequacy and effectiveness, both for preparing and dealing with possible liquidity crisis, should be regularly verified and a specific analysis performed and results presented to the board of directors at least annually. As we shall set up and maintain these contingencies, indicating the strategies for addressing liquidity needs during liquidity stress events, plans need to be commensurate with the company's business structure, its set risk profile and liquidity risk tolerance. The analysis should address the full range of aspects, including legal terms, funds transferability, stress testing in fire sales in terms of price impacts, reputational impacts and modified market conditions. An additional test will be to implement a contingency plan in full in one of the controlled legal entities and see whether it works as expected.

5.5.1 Outlining the contingency funding plans

The CFP is the follow-on step from the stress test and the means by which the organization mitigates the risks identified in the stress tests so as to reduce them to fit within its risk appetite. We are expected to include in the contingency funding plan:

- Policies and procedures to effectively manage a range of stresses, including structured decision-making processes and a detailed description of roles and responsibilities in dedicated internal rules.
- An articulated description of different, and as uncorrelated as possible, sets of viable, readily available and flexible additional funding measures to obtain liquidity and offset sudden cash outfalls.
- Quantification of funds one can obtain from these contingency funding sources, and the maximum time required to get these.
- Estimation of the economic and business impacts of the contingency plan implementation.
- Appropriate communication procedures addressing the internal and press information in case of contingency triggering.
- The necessary steps to meet critical payments, also intraday when liquidity resources become limited or there could be payment and settlement difficulties.
- Rules to ensure timely and clear information reporting to the company's board and senior management on the plan implementation and its results.

In ensuring the contingency funding plan is sound, we need to apply set assumptions and possible outcomes:

- The impact of stressed market conditions on its ability to sell or dispose of assets.
- The extensive or complete loss of normally available funding sources.

- Business and reputational consequences of the execution of such a contingency plan.
- The capacity to transfer liquidity within the controlled legal entities, given legal, regulatory or operational limitations.
- Central bank liquidity facility access.

5.5.2 Internal procedures for CFP

The two components of the contingency plan are first the risk tolerance set and the degree of securities buffer resulting, and second – and as important – are the internal procedures triggered by the plan. We would envisage that the bank CFP relied on a contingency funding plan policy articulated by a dedicated CFP committee, responsible for those circumstances when funding emergencies are triggered.

The CFP emergency committee will be convened in specific market conditions; it will include limited key managers at the highest managerial level and be called weekly, at least. The agenda and minutes should be part of the CFP policy, while market intervention will depend on the conditions and specific circumstances.

CHAPTER **6**

Conclusions

The idea of this book came from a discussion with the publishers on what might be relevant topics, and then, as now, liquidity risk is a particularly interesting one. I took the proposal a bit further, coming from a period of extremely difficult markets and refinancing conditions, and decided it was preferable and surely more interesting to focus on the funding side of the liquidity risk. I do not know whether in a few years this will be as immediate as it is now, markets and economic conditions are changing and the European Union, where I have direct working experience and can present some insights, is undergoing the most severe recession since the second world war, likely since the 1929 crisis: industrial growth is declining in most of the EU members and so is employment. Mario Draghi, currently chairing the European Central Bank, has further curbed official rates, thus bringing them to extremely low levels, with one side hoping to boost investment and recovery, and the other increasingly presenting the EU with the challenge of boosting the economy and controlling inflation levels.

6.1 FUNDING LIQUIDITY

There has been substantial work within the industry and by supervisors. The first Basel liquidity frameworks, following extensive quantitative impact studies, have been reviewed and substantially improved: the two ratio components and their weights are now different, monitoring requirements and intraday are also now in a revised form. In the meantime, central banks have taken several initiatives to improve market liquidity, hoping to re-launch economies and ensuring there are the conditions necessary to boost banks' lending and thus ensure economic growth. In many countries, market liquidity conditions have returned to their normal, pre-crisis, levels. Some structural changes have also occurred:

- The central bank's role in providing systemic facilities (namely, US federal reserve quantitative easing and the ECB's long-term refinancing operation).
- Collateralized or asset-backed securities have substantially replaced uncollateralized interbank lending.
- Financial institution building of large buffers of high-quality liquid assets, mainly bonds.
- Liquidity risk monitoring as a daily, regular routine, including stress testing.

6.2 PROFITABILITY IMPACT OF LARGER COUNTERBALANCING ASSET STOCKS

The regulatory response to funding liquidity risk has been a focus on the larger, higher credit quality stock of securities held for counterbalancing and liquidity needs, together with a strict balance of cash inflows and outflows to the longer maturity and main currencies. This, irrespective of interest rate changes and curve shapes, will have an impact on banks' long-term revenue capacity. It might refuel merger sprees or the spawning of smaller, regional, cooperative types of lenders. Whether this is a positive effect remains to be seen once the rate levels and shapes, together with inflation, shift upwards.

6.3 PRICING AND LIQUIDITY

The effect of liquidity on financial instrument prices is regaining attention, following increased requirements from regulators and accounting standards (e.g. IFRS and EBA). The effect of holding a large quantity of specific assets or the impact of illiquid instruments needs to be better assessed and valued. The industry is therefore moving into adjustments for such elements, in addition to others such as market price uncertainties, resulting in fair value or additional value adjustments. Risk control and accounting functions will then have to determine such liquidity adjustments for individual positions and provide evidence of changes on a monthly basis.

6.4 LESSONS LEARNT

Whether funding for banks will again be a key risk factor is unclear; all the analysis and indications presented might soon become obsolete or just a bad historical memory. The lessons learnt will remain valid though: the way banks suddenly found the unsecured money market draining and very rapidly disappearing, the relaxed attitude towards asset growth and the pyramid mechanisms relying on self-securitization are likely never to be repeated, and in any case their history has been traced and is available for future risk valuation.

Bibliography

Acharya, V. and Pedersen, L., 2005, "Asset pricing with liquidity risk", *Journal of Financial Economics* 77, 375–410.

Admati, A. and Pfleiderer, P., 1988, "Theory of intraday patterns: Volume and price variability", *Review of Financial Studies* 1, 3–40.

Affleck-Graves, J., Callahan, C., and Chipalkatti, N., 2002, "Earnings predictability, information asymmetry, and market liquidity", *Journal of Accounting Research* 40, 561–583.

Allen, F. and Gale, D., 2000 "Financial contagion", *Journal of Political Economy* 108 (1), 1–33.

Allen, F. and Gale, D., 2004, "Financial fragility, liquidity and asset prices", *Journal of the European Economic Association* 2 (6), 1015–1048.

Allen, F. and Gale, D., 2004, "Financial intermediaries and markets", *Econometrica* 72 (4), 1012–1061.

Allen, F. and Gale, D., 2007, *Understanding Financial Crises*, Oxford University Press.

Amihud, Y., 2002, "Illiquidity and stock returns: Cross-section and time-series effects", *Journal of Financial Markets* 5, 31–56.

Amihud, Y. and Mendelson, H., 1986, "Asset pricing and the bid-ask spread", *Journal of Financial Economics* 17, 223–249.

Amihud, Y. and Mendelson, H., 1988, "Liquidity and asset prices: financial management implications", *Financial Management* 17 (1), 5–15.

Amihud, Y. and Mendelson, H., 1991, "Liquidity, asset prices and financial policy", *Financial Analysts Journal* 47 (6), 56–66.

Amihud, Y., Mendelson, H., and Lauterbach, B., 1997, "Market microstructure and securities values: evidence from the Tel Aviv Exchange", *Journal of Financial Economics* 45, 365–390.

Asness, C.S., 1997, "The interaction of value and momentum strategies", *Financial Analysts Journal* (March/April), 29–36.

Ausubel, L., 2004, "An efficient ascending-bid auction for multiple objects", *American Economic Review* 94 (5), 1452–1475.

Ayusi, J. and Repullo, R., 2003, "A model of the open market operations of the European Central Bank", *Economic Journal* 113, 883–902.

Ball, R. and Bartov, E., 1996, "How naive is the stock market's use of earning information", *Journal of Accounting and Economics* 21, 319–337.

Banks, E., 2005, *Liquidity Risk: Managing Asset and Funding Risk*, Palgrave Macmillan.

Bao, J. and Wang, J., 2011, "The illiquidity of corporate bonds", *The Journal of Finance* 66, 911–946.

Barberis, N., Shleifer, A., and Vishny, R., 1998, "A model of investor sentiment", *Journal of Financial Economics* 49, 307–343.

Barclay, M.J. and Hendershott, T., 2004, "Liquidity externalities and adverse selection: evidence from trading after hours", *Journal of Finance* 58, 681–710.

Basel Committee on Banking Supervision 2008, *Principles for Sound Liquidity Risk Management and Supervision*.

Berkman, H. and Eleswarapu, V., 1998, "Short–term traders and liquidity: a test using Bombay Stock Exchange data", *Journal of Financial Economics* 47, 339–355.

Bernard, V.L. and Thomas, J.K., 1989, "Post-earnings announcement drift and delayed price response or risk premium?" *Journal of Accounting Research* 27, 1–36.

Bernard, V.L. and Thomas, J.K., 1990, "Evidence that stock prices do not fully reflect the implications of current earnings for future earnings", *Journal of Accounting and Economics* 13, 305–340.

Bindseil, U., Weller, B., and Wuertz, F., 2003, "Central banks and commercial banks' liquidity risk management", *Economic Notes* 32 (1), 37–66.

Brennan, M.J. and Subrahmanyam, A., 1996, "Market microstructure and asset pricing: On the compensation for illiquidity in stock returns", *Journal of Financial Economics* 41, 441–464.

Campbell, J.Y. and Kyle, A.S., 1993, "Smart money, noise trading and stock price behavior", *Review of Economic Studies* 60, 1–34.

Cao, C., Field, L., and Hanka, G., 2004, "Does insider trading impair market liquidity? Evidence from IPO lockup expirations", *Journal of Financial and Quantitative Analysis* 39, 25–46.

Chan, L.K.C., Jegadeesh, N., and Lakonishok, J., 1996, "Momentum strategies", *Journal of Finance* 51, 1681–1713.

Chan, W.S., 2003, "Stock price reaction to news and no-news: drift and reversal after headlines", *Journal of Financial Economics* 70, 223–260.

Chen, N-F., Roll, R., and Ross, S.A., 1986, "Economic forces and the stock market", *Journal of Business* 59, 383–403.

Chordia, T., Roll, R., and Subrahmanyam, A., 2000, "Commonality in liquidity", *Journal of Financial Economics* 56, 3–28.

Chordia, T., Roll, R., and Subrahmanyam, A., 2001, "Market liquidity and trading activity", *Journal of Finance* 56, 501–530.

Chordia, T., Roll, R., and Subrahmanyam, A., 2002, "Order imbalance, liquidity and market returns", *Journal of Financial Economics*, 65, 111–130.

Chordia, T., Sarkar, A., and Subrahmanyam, A., 2005, "An empirical analysis of stock and bond market liquidity", *The Review of Financial Studies* 18(1), 85–128.

Christie, W. and Schultz, P., 1994, "Why do NASDAQ market makers avoid odd-eighth quotes?", *Journal of Finance* 49, 1813–1840.

Cohen, R.B., Polk, C., and Vuolteenaho, T., 2003, "The value spread", *Journal of Finance* 58, 609–641.

Cooper, S., Groth, K., and Avera, W., 1985, "Liquidity, exchange listing and common stock performance", *Journal of Economics and Business* 37, 19–33.

Daniel, K., Hirshleifer, D., and Subrahmanyam, A., 1998, "Investor psychology and security market under and overreactions", *Journal of Finance* 53, 1839–1886.

De Bondt, W. and Thaler, R., 1985, "Does the stock market overreact?", *Journal of Finance* 40, 793–805.

De Long, J. B., Shleifer, S., Summers, L.H., and Waldmann, R.J, 1990, "Noise trader risk in financial markets", *Journal of Political Economy* 98, 703–738.

Dennis, P. and Strickland, D., 2003, "The effect of stock splits on liquidity: evidence from shareholder ownership composition", *Journal of Financial Research* 26, 355–370.

Diamond, D.W. and Rajan, R.G., 2005, "Liquidity shortages and banking crises", *Journal of Finance* 60 (2), 615–647.

Dick-Nielsen, J. and Feldhutter, L.D., 2012, "Corporate bond liquidity before and after the onset of the subprime crisis", *Journal of Financial Economics* 109, 471–492.

Easley, D., Hvidkjaer, S., and O'Hara, M., 2002, "Is information risk a determinant of asset returns?", *The Journal of Finance* 58, 2185–2210.

Eisfeldt, A.L., 2004, "Endogenous liquidity in asset markets", *Journal of Finance* 59, 1–30.

Ellis, K., Michaely, R., and O'Hara, M., 2000, "The accuracy of trade classification rules: Evidence from Nasdaq", *Journal of Financial and Quantitative Analysis* 35, 529–551.

Fama, E.F., 1998, "Market efficiency, long-term returns, and behavioral finance", *Journal of Financial Economics* 49, 283–306.

Fama, E.F. and French, K.R., 1993, "Common risk factors in the returns on stocks and bonds", *Journal of Financial Economics* 33, 3–56.

Fama, E.F. and French, K.R., 1996, "Multifactor explanations of asset pricing anomalies", *Journal of Finance* 51, 55–84.

Fama, E.F. and MacBeth, J., 1973, "Risk, return and equilibrium: empirical tests", *Journal of Political Economy* 81, 607–636.

Flannery, M.J., 1996, "Financial crises, payment system problems, and discount window lending", *Journal of Money, Credit and Banking* 28 (4), 804–824.

Foster, F.D., and Viswanathan, S., 1993, "Variation in trading volume, return volatility, and trading costs: evidence on recent price formation models", *Journal of Finance* 48, 187–211.

Foster, G., Olsen, C., and Shevlin, T., 1984, "Earnings releases, anomalies, and the behavior of security returns", *The Accounting Review* 59, 574–603.

Furfine, C., 2002, "The interbank market during a crisis", *European Economic Review* 46 (4–5), 809–820.

Gatev, E. and Strahan, P.E., 2006, "Banks' advantage in hedging liquidity risk: theory and evidence from the commercial paper market", *Journal of Finance* 61(2), 867–892.

George, T.J., Gautum, K., and Nimalendran, M., 1991, "Estimation of the bid-ask spread and its components: A new approach", *Review of Financial Studies* 4, 623–656.

Glosten, L.R., 1987, "Components of the bid-ask spread and the statistical properties of transaction prices", *Journal of Finance* 42, 1293–1307.

Glosten, L.R. and Harris, L.E., 1988, "Estimating the components of the bid/ask spread", *Journal of Financial Economics* 21, 123–142.

Gondat-Larralde, C. and Nier, E., 2004, "The economics of retail banking – an empirical analysis of the UK market for personal current accounts", *Bank of England Quarterly Bulletin*, Spring.

Grundy, B.D. and Spencer Martin, J., 2001, "Understanding the nature of the risks and the sources of the rewards to momentum investing", *Review of Financial Studies* 14, 29–78.

Gyntelberg, J. and Wooldridge, P., 2008, "Interbank rate fixings during the recent turmoil", *BIS Quarterly Review*, 59–72.

Hansen, L.P., 1982, "Large sample properties of generalized method of moments estimators", *Econometrica* 50, 1029–1054.

Hansen, L.P., and Jagannathan, R., 1997, "Assessing specification errors in stochastic discount factor models", *Journal of Finance* 62, 557–590.

Harris, L., 1991, "Stock price clustering and discreteness", *Review of Financial Studies* 4, 389–415.

Hasbrouck, J., 1991, "Measuring the information content of stock trades", *Journal of Finance* 46, 179–207.

Hasbrouck, J., 1999, "The dynamics of discrete bid and ask quotes", *Journal of Finance* 54, 2109–2142.

Helfin, F. and Shaw, K., 2000, "Blockholder ownership and market liquidity", *Journal of Financial and Quantitative Analysis* 35, 621–633.

Holmström, B. and Tirole, J., 2001. "LAPM: A liquidity-based asset pricing model", *The Journal of Finance* 56 (5), 1837–1867.

Huang, R. and Stoll, H., 1996, "Dealer versus auction markets: A paired comparison of execution costs on NASDAQ and the NYSE", *Journal of Financial Economics* 41, 313–357.

Huang, R. and Stoll, H., 1997, "The components of the bid-ask spread: A general approach", *Review of Financial Studies* 10, 995–1034.

Jagannathan, R. and Wang, Z., 1996, "The conditional CAPM and the cross–section of expected returns", *Journal of Finance* 51, 3–53.

Jarrow, R. and van Deventer, D., 1998, "The arbitrage-free valuation and hedging of demand deposits and credit card loans", *Journal of Banking and Finance* 22, 249–272.

Jegadeesh, N. and Titman, S., 1993, "Returns to buying winners and selling losers: implications for market efficiency", *Journal of Finance* 48, 65–92.

Jegadeesh, N. and Titman, S., 2001, "Profitability of momentum strategies: an evaluation of alternative explanations", *Journal of Finance* 56, 699–720.

Jones, C.P. and Litzenberger, R.H., 1970, "Quarterly earnings reports and intermediate stock price trends", *Journal of Finance* 25 (1), 143–148.

Joy, O.M., Litzenberger, R.H., and McEnally, R.W., 1977, "The adjustment of stock prices to announcements of unanticipated changes in quarterly earnings", *Journal of Accounting Research* 15, 207–225.

Kalev, P., Pham, P., and Steen, A., 2003, "Underpricing, stock allocation, ownership structure and post-listing liquidity of newly listed firms", *Journal of Banking and Finance* 27, 919–947.

Kashyap, A., Rajan, R.G., and Stein, J.C., 2002, "Banks as liquidity providers: An explanation for the coexistence of lending and deposit-taking", *Journal of Finance* 57 (1), 33–73.

Keim, D.B. and Madhavan, A., 1996, "The upstairs market for large-block transactions: analysis and measurement of price effects", *Review of Financial Studies* 9, 1–36.

Keim, D. and Madhavan, A., 1997, "Transactions costs and investment style: An interexchange analysis of institutional equity trades", *Journal of Financial Economics* 46, 265–292.

Kim, D. and Myung-Sun, K., 2003, "A multifactor explanation of post-earnings-announcement drift", *Journal of Financial and Quantitative Analysis* 38, 383–398.

Knez, P.J. and Ready, M.J., 1996, "Estimating the profits from trading strategies", *Review of Financial Studies* 9, 1121–1163.

Korajczyk, R.A. and Sadka, R., 2004, "Are momentum profits robust to trading costs?", *Journal of Finance* 59, 1039–1082.

Korajczyk, R.A. and Sadka, R., 2008, "Pricing the commonality across alternative measures of liquidity", *Journal of Financial Economics* 87, 45–72.

Kyle, A.S., 1985, "Continuous auctions and insider trading", *Econometrica* 53, 1315–1335.

Lee, C. and Radhakrishna, B., 2000, "Inferring investor behavior: Evidence from TORQ data", *Journal of Financial Markets* 3, 83–112.

Lee, C.M.C. and Ready, M.J., 1991, "Inferring trade direction from intra-day data", *Journal of Finance* 46, 733–746.

Lee, C.M.C., Mucklow, B., and Ready, M.J., 1993, "Spreads, depths, and the impact of earnings information: an intraday analysis", *Review of Financial Studies* 6, 345–374.

Lerner, J. and Schoar, A., 2004, "The illiquidity puzzle: Theory and evidence from private equity", *Journal of Financial Economics* 72, 3–40.

Lesmond, D., Ogden, J., and Trzcinka, C., 1999, A new estimate of transaction costs, *Review of Financial Studies* 12, 1113–1141.

Lesmond, D. A., Schill, M.J., and Zhou, C., 2004, The illusory nature of momentum profits, *Journal of Financial Economics* 71, 349–380.

Liu, H., 2004, "Optimal consumption and investment with transaction costs and multiple risky assets", *Journal of Finance* 59, 289–338.

Madhavan, A. and Smidt, S., 1991, "A Bayesian model of intraday specialist pricing", *Journal of Financial Economics* 30, 99–134.

Madhavan, A., Richardson, M., and Roomans, M., 1997, "Why do security prices change? A transaction-level analysis of NYSE stocks", *Review of Financial Studies* 10, 1035–1064.

Marshall, B., Nguyen, N.H., and Visaltanachoti, N., 2013, "Commodity liquidity measurement and transaction costs", *The Review of Financial Studies* 25, 599–638.

Matz, L. and Neu, P., 2006, *Liquidity Risk: Measurement and Management*, Wiley.

Mendenhall, R., 2004, "Arbitrage risk and post-earnings-announcement drift", *Journal of Business* 77, 875–894.

Michaud, F.-L. and Upper, C., 2008, "What drives interbank rates? Evidence from the Libor panel", *BIS Quarterly Review*, 47–58.

Mitchell, M. and Pulvino, T., 2001, "Characteristics of risk and return in risk arbitrage", *Journal of Finance* 56, 2135–2175.

Moskowitz, T.J. and Grinblatt, M., 1999, "Do industries explain momentum?", *Journal of Finance* 54, 1249–1290.

Nyborg, K.G. and Strebulaev, I.A., 2004, "Multiple unit auctions and short squeezes", *The Review of Financial Studies* 17 (2), 545–580.

Odders-White, E.R., 2000, "On the occurrence and consequences of inaccurate trade classification", *Journal of Financial Markets* 3, 259–286.

Pastor, L. and Stambaugh, R., 2003, "Liquidity risk and expected stock returns", *Journal of Political Economy* 111, 642–685.

Pennacchi, G., 2006, "Deposit insurance, bank regulation and financial system risk", *Journal of Monetary Economics* 53, 1–30.

Persaud, A., 2006, "Investors' shifting appetite for risk", FX research note, Morgan Guaranty Trust Co., NY.

Peterson, M. and Sirri, E., 2003, "Evaluation of the biases in execution costs estimation using trades and quotes data", *Journal of Financial Markets* 6, 259–280.

Poole, W., 1968, "Commercial bank reserve management in a stochastic model: Implications for monetary policy", *Journal of Finance*, December, 769–791.

Rendleman, R.J. Jr., Jones, C.P., and Latané, H.A., 1982, "Empirical anomalies based on unexpected earnings and the importance of risk adjustments", *Journal of Financial Economics* 10, 269–287.

Rochet, J.C. and Vives, X., 2004, "Coordination failures and the lender of last resort: Was Bagehot right after all?", *Journal of the European Economic Association* 2 (6), 1116–1147.

Roll, R., 1984. "A simple implicit measure of the effective bid-ask spread in an efficient market", *Journal of Finance* 39, 1127–1139.

Rouwenhorst, G., 1998, "International momentum strategies", *Journal of Finance* 53, 267–284.

Sadka, R., 2006, "Liquidity risk and asset pricing", *Journal of Financial Economics* 80, 309–349.

Schultz, P., 2000, "Regulatory and legal pressures and the costs of Nasdaq trading", *Review of Financial Studies* 13, 917–957.

Shanken, J., 1992, "On the estimation of beta-pricing models", *Review of Financial Studies* 5, 1–33.

Stiglitz, J. and Weiss, A., 1981, "Credit rationing in markets with imperfect information", *American Economic Review* 71 (3), 393–410.

Valimaki, T., 2006. "Why the marginal MRO rate exceeds the ECB policy rate", Bank of Finland, Research Discussion Papers 200/2006.

Wagner, W., 2011, "Systemic liquidation risk and the diversity–diversification trade-off", *The Journal of Finance* 66, 1141–1175.

Wurgler, J. and Zhuravskaya, K., 2002, "Does arbitrage flatten demand curve for stocks?", *Journal of Business* 75, 583–608.

Index

2007–08 crisis 6

accounting classification of
   products 31
ADS BCI (Arouba Diebold Scotti
   Business Conditions Index)
   62–63
ALM (asset liability
   management) 94
Amihud and Mendelson model
   89
Arouba Diebold Scotti Business
   Conditions Index (ADS BCI)
   62–63
ASF (available stable funding)
   factor 96
asks 138
asset liability management
   (ALM) 94
asset liquidity measurement
   87–91
assets
   documentation-related liquidity
      risks 154
   first-level 47–48
   'high quality' 18–19
   levels 46–51

liquid assets 46–51
liquidation-adjusted VaR 135
liquidity cover ratio 46–51
liquidity measurement 87–91
liquidity risk 5–6, 8
market liquidity 125–126
refinancing 46–51, 156–157
required stable funding for
   97–99
second-level 49–51
types graph 47
asset stocks profitability 170
assumptions modelling 106–108
available stable funding (ASF)
   factor 96

back/front office functions 67–68
balance, long-term 93–122
balance sheet contingency plan
   164
banks/banking
   assumptions modelling
      107–108
   cash-flow ladder 39–40
   contingency funding plan 166
   correspondent banking 30–31,
      77

banks/banking (*Continued*)
counterbalancing capacity 4,
20, 77
customer deposit modelling
100–101
depositor behaviours 105
deposit stability 103–104
funding 23–26
governance principles 143–144,
146, 148
interbank fund payment
systems 70
intraday liquidity management
67–68
market liquidity 125–126
refinancing funds 16–19
required stable funding for
assets 97
risk management framework
9–14
scenario analysis 120
settlement banks 69–71, 73–75
stress testing 111–113,
118–119
structural funding 94–95
Value at Risk 128
wholesale banks 22
Basel 2.5, liquidity risk horizons
139
Basel 3
contractual cash flows 40
liquidity risk indicators 59
long-term funding requirements
22–23
market liquidity 16, 18
reverse stress testing 119
total net cash outflows 21

Basel Committee on Banking
Supervision (BCBS) 15–17,
52–53, 56, 138, 143–144
behavioural changes, customers
28–29
see also customer behaviour;
depositor behaviours
bid-ask spreads 88, 124,
127–129, 131
bids 138
board roles 112–113, 149
bonds *see* government bond yield
curves; zero-coupon bonds

capital, stress testing 122
cash-flow ladder 37–45
contractual cash flows 40
flows without contractual
certainty 42–43
key elements 38–39
mapping onto ladder 41–42
refinancing funds 44
short-term funding 37–45
total ladder calculation 44–45
transferability of fund 44
unexpected cash flows 43
cash flows 140–141, 155
cash inflows 56–58
cash outflows 21–22, 51–58
CDSs (credit default swaps) 61
central banks 5–6, 62, 104
see also banks/banking
centralized liquidity management
152–153
CFP *see* contingency funding
plan
Chief Risk Officers (CROs) 15

Citigroup Surprise index 64
client securities regulatory
    frameworks 21
    see also customers; investors
close-out netting 29–30
CLS (continuous linked
    settlement) system 31
collateral, additional 55
collateral management 155
collateral posting 147, 154–155
commercial network transactions
    43
communication, depositor
    behaviours 106
company-specific information
    160
complex financial derivatives
    25–26
concentration of funding sources
    83–87, 157
confidence crises 8
contagion risks 83, 126
contingency funding
    control processes 152
    governance principles 147–148
    obligations, cash outflows 56
contingency funding plan (CFP)
    164–168
contingency plans 33–35,
    164–168
contingent liability exposures
    40
continuous linked settlement
    (CLS) system 31
contracts, covenants 27
contractual cash flows 40
contractual loans 56

contractual uncertainty, cash-flow
    ladder 43
control function staff, banks 11
controls
    see also internal control
    framework 143–168
    governance principles 143–148
    improving 117
    liquidity risk 150–151
    processes 148–155
cooperative mechanism, intraday
    liquidity risk 71, 73, 74, 75
coordinating liquidity
    management 152–153
core level, non-maturity deposits
    102
Cornish–Fisher expansion 129
corporate depositor behaviour
    104
correspondent banking 30–31, 77
costs
    assumptions modelling and
        106–108
    liquidation-adjusted VaR 135
    of liquidity 146
    market liquidity 123, 128, 132
    non-maturity deposits 102
counterbalancing asset stocks 170
counterbalancing capacity 4, 20,
    77, 148
counterparties, funding
    concentration 85–86
covenants funding 27–28
coverage ratio 95
    see also liquidity
        cover/coverage ratio
credit crunch 74–75

credit default swaps (CDSs) 61
credit lines
  cash inflows 57
  cash outflows 55–56
  intraday liquidity risk 81
creditors, covenants 27
credit risk limits 161
credit spread information 159
creditworthiness, funding 83
crises
  2007–08 crisis 6
  confidence 8–9
  customer deposit modelling 103
  market liquidity 126
  scenario analysis 120
crisis indicators
  intraday liquidity management
    69
  liquidity risk 62–64
crisis management, contingency
    plans 33–35, 165
CROs (Chief Risk Officers) 15
cross-spreads 61
currencies 58, 86–87, 157–158
custody activities 30–31
customer behaviour
  changes 28–29
  interest rates and 108
customer deposit modelling
    99–111
customers
  see also client...
  governance principles 146
  intraday liquidity risk 81

data quality, stress testing 115
debt market information 159

deep markets 131–132
demand deposits 109, 111
deposit modelling 99–111
depositor behaviours 104–106
deposit stability 53–54, 103–104
derivatives 25–26, 32–33, 55, 58,
    116
discounted cash flows 111
distribution of reporting 160–161
diversification 147
diversified funding sources 31–32
documentary frameworks 149
documentation-related liquidity
    risks 154–155
documentation risk 28
dynamic regression models
    109–111

ECB (European Central Bank) 6
economies of scale 137
endogenous liquidity risk 132,
    137–138
escalation procedures 163
estimated net return variance
    (EWMA) 130
Eurocoin Growth Indicator, New
    Eurocoin index 63
European Central Bank (ECB) 6
event analysis, stress testing 118
EWMA (estimated net return
    variance) 130
execution lag,
    liquidation-adjusted VaR 136
exogenous liquidity risk 132,
    137–138
exposures 154, 155–161
extreme shocks 120–121

financial sector information 159
first-level assets 47–48
flexibility, stress testing 114
forecasting intraday liquidity risk
  80
foreign exchange indicators
  61–62
forward-looking outcomes, stress
  testing 118
frequency of reporting 160–161
front/back office functions 67–68
funding concentration 83–87,
  157
  high risk examples 84
  key elements 85
  significant counterparties 85–86
  significant currencies 86–87
  significant products 86
  time buckets 87
funding/funds 1–35, 169–170
  see also short-term funding
  cash flow ladder 44
  costs, assumptions modelling
    106–108
  counterbalancing capacity 148
  customer deposit modelling
    100–103
  definitions 4–9
  determining availability 95–96
  diversification of sources 31–32
  factors driving liquidity 24
  liquidity risk 4–15, 37, 148
  long-term balance 93–99
  long-term requirements 22–23
  market liquidity 1–35, 124–126,
    148
  for refinancing 44

regulatory frameworks 15–35
reporting frequency/distribution
  161
risks 4–15, 37, 116, 147–148
through securitization 26–28
transferability 44
in various currencies 157–158

GDP (gross domestic product) 63
Germany ZEW indicator of
  economic sentiment 63
Global Risk Aversion Index
  (GRAI) 65–66
governance principles 143–148
government bond yield curves 61
GRAI (Global Risk Aversion
  Index) 65–66
granular testing 117
gross domestic product (GDP) 63

haircuts 50, 75–76, 156
hedging strategies 108
highest quality assets, LCR 49
high quality assets/securities 18,
  19, 46–47, 51
holding period, VaR
  liquidation-adjusted 133–134
hypothetical stress testing 114

ICAAP (internal capital adequacy
  assessment process) 122
ILQ (market illiquidity) 90
inflationary rates 107
information gathering
  company-specific 160
  financial sector 159
  markets 158–159

interbank fund payment systems 70
interbank lending, market liquidity 126
interest rate risk 107–108
interest rates, non-maturity deposits 101–102, 108–109
internal capital adequacy assessment process (ICAAP) 122
internal capital, stress testing 122
internal control, liquidity risk 13–14
internal procedures, CFP 168
internal rules, liquidity risk limit setting 164
internet accounts 106
interval structures, cash-flow ladder 39–40
intraday credit lines 81
intraday liquidity management 67–71
intraday liquidity risk 66–82, 147
    cooperative mechanism 71, 73, 74, 75
    critical obligations 81
    haircuts to pledges 75–78
    Lehman Brothers 79
    liquidity buffers 77–78
    liquidity management 67–71
    liquidity optimization mechanisms 78–79
    maximum liquidity requirement 80–81
    monitoring 76, 80–82
    payments ensured on behalf of customers 81

stress scenarios 73–75, 82
structural/liquidity needs 76–78
timing of payments 82
intraday payment system 29
investment, off-balance sheet 26
investors' behavioural changes 28–29

Jarrow and van Deventer model 109–111

kurtosis, market liquidity 129

larger counterbalancing asset stocks 170
LA-VaR (liquidation-adjusted VaR) 133–140
LCR see liquidity cover/coverage ratio
legal constraints, monitoring 155
legal entities 152–153, 166
Lehman Brothers 19–20, 77, 79
Level 1 assets 47–48
Level 2A/2B assets 49–51
liabilities, elements 94–95
limit maps, liquidity 163
limit order book, market liquidity 130–131
liquidation-adjusted VaR (LA-VaR) 133–140
liquidity cost component, non-maturity deposits 102
liquidity cover/coverage ratio (LCR) 45–58
    see also coverage ratio
    assets for refinancing 46–51
    calculation of 45, 51

cash inflows 56–58
cash outflows 51–56
countries graph 48
governance principles 144
market liquidity 16–20, 22
regulatory prescriptions 45–46
reporting frequency/distribution
  161
setting limits 162
total net cash outflows in
  upcoming month 51–58
in various currencies 157–158
liquidity horizons, definition
  139
liquidity ladder *see* cash-flow
  ladder
liquidity optimization
  mechanisms 78–79
liquidity risk 2–15
  appetite for 144–145
  calculation 128
  Chief Risk Officers 15
  definition 4–9
  framework 9–14
  functions in charge of 150–151
  funding 4, 26–27, 37
  horizons 138–140
  intraday 66–82
  management 9–15, 144, 164
  market liquidity 2–9
  monitoring function 153, 155
  rating agencies 32
  setting limits 161–164
  short-term funding 37–38,
    58–66
  transparency 32–33
  understanding 148

liquidity risk control 112
  see also stress testing
liquidity risk indicators 58–66
  central bank refinancing 62
  credit default swap levels 61
  crisis indicators 62–64
  critical issues 60
  cross-spreads 61
  foreign exchange cross-values
    61–62
  government bond yield curves
    61
  risk aversion indexes 65–66
  testing 60
  using indicators 59–60
long-term balance 93–122
  customer deposit modelling
    99–111
  dynamic regression models
    109–111
  scenario analysis 111–122
  stress testing 111–122
  structural funding 94–99
long-term funding 22–23

managerial limits, liquidity risk
  161–162
managing liquidity risk 9–15,
  144, 164
market contingency plan 164
market funding 23–24
market illiquidity (ILQ) 90
market information 158–159
market interest rates 108
market liquidity 1–35, 123–132,
  140
market order types 124

market-related monitoring tools 158
market risk 7, 127, 161
market volatility 27, 124
mark-to-market value, non-maturity deposits 107
mass market depositors 104–105
maturing assets 94
maturity, assumptions modelling 107
maturity ladders 42, 141
measurement framework, governance 146
Mendelson *see* Amihud and Mendelson
mid prices, market liquidity 131
money market accounts, Jarrow and van Deventer model 110
monitoring
  intraday liquidity risk 76, 80–82
  liquidity exposure 155–161
  liquidity risk 153, 155
  process recommendations 160
mutual trust, cooperative mechanism 71, 73, 75

net present value, dynamic regression models 111
net stable funding ratio (NSFR) 157–158, 161, 162
netting payment systems 29–30
non-asset-backed market access 159
non-maturity deposits 101–102, 107, 108, 109
Northern Rock bank 76
NSFR *see* net stable funding ratio

off-balance sheet exposures 97, 99
off-balance sheet facilities, cash outflows 55–56
off-balance sheet investments 26
operational constraints, monitoring 155
operational limits, liquidity risk 161, 163
organizational structures, liquidity risk management 150
originate-to-distribute model 24, 125
outflows, total net cash 21–22
oversight, liquidity risk 153

payments 29–30, 67–79
permanent market impact, liquidation-adjusted VaR 134
pledges, haircuts 75–76
policies, control processes 149
portfolio value, VaR liquidation-adjusted 133, 135–136
power delegation, liquidity risk management 151
price impact costs, market liquidity 128
price movement, liquidation-adjusted VaR 134, 135–136
prices/pricing
  liquidation-adjusted VaR 134
  of liquidity 145–146, 171
  market liquidity 127, 129, 131
price volatility, market liquidity 126

profitability impact,
    counterbalancing asset stocks
    170
profit/service centres distinction
    149

qualitative approaches, risk
    management 12
quantitative requirements,
    contingency plans 33

rating agencies, liquidity risk 32
ratios *see* coverage ratio; liquidity
    cover/coverage ratio; net
    stable funding ratio; standard
    liquidity ratio
real-time payment systems 29
refinancing
    assets available for 46–51,
       156–157
    cash-flow ladder 44
    central banks 62
    funds 16–19, 44
    liquidity risk indicators 62
    risk 2–3
regression models, long-term
    balance 109–111
regulatory approaches/aspects 38,
    103–104
regulatory frameworks
    accounting treatment 31
    bank funding 23–26
    contingency plans 33–35
    correspondent banking 30–31
    custody activities 30–31
    customer behavioural changes
       28–29

diversified funding sources
    31–32
funding 15–35
long-term funding requirements
    22–23
market liquidity 15–35
payment systems 29–30
rating agencies 32
total net cash outflows 21–22
transparency 32–33
regulatory limits, liquidity risk
    161
remuneration policies, banks
    10–11
remuneration systems 146
reporting
    cash-flow ladder 39–40
    frequency/distribution 160–161
    procedures 163
    requirements 156–157,
       160–161
    risk management 12–13
reputational exposure 74
reputation risk funding 5, 7
required stable funding (RSF)
    factor 97–99
resilience modelling, customer
    deposits 100–102
resiliency, market liquidity 132
retail customer behavioural
    changes 28–29
retail deposit funding 23
retail funding 23, 100
reverse stress testing 118–119
reviews, liquidity risk limit
    setting 162–163
risk aversion indices 65–66

risk committees 151–152
risk control 68, 153
risk factors 129–130, 139–140
risk governance, bank stress
    testing 112–113
risk management
  control processes 148, 150–151
  governance principles 144–145
  liquidity risk 9–15
risk mitigation 119
risk models, scenario analysis 121
risks
  see also individual risks;
    liquidity risk…; risk…
  cash flows at risk 140–141
  liquidity funding 116
  market liquidity 123, 126–127
roll out assumptions, cash-flow
    ladder 43
Roll spread measures 90–91
RSF (required stable funding)
    factor 97–99

savings funding 101–103
scenario analysis 12, 25, 111–122
second-level assets 49–51
securities 18–19, 21
securitization, funding 26–28
senior management, banks
    112–113
sensitivity analysis, stress testing
    118
service centres/profit distinction
    149
settlement
  banks 69–71, 73–75
  CLS system 31

intraday liquidity management
    69–71, 73–75
  payment systems 29–30
shocks, scenario analysis
    120–121
short-term funding 37–91
  asset liquidity measurement
    87–91
  cash-flow ladder 37–45
  funding concentration 83–87
  intraday liquidity risk 66–82
  liquidity cover ratio 45–58
  liquidity risk indicators 58–66
sight deposit market 109
sights funding 101–103
skewness, market liquidity 129
SLR (standard liquidity ratio)
    89–90
small businesses 54–55, 58
spreads 90–91, 124, 127–129,
    131–132, 137–138, 159
stable fraction, non-maturity
    deposits 102
stable funding 96–99, 157–158,
    161
standard liquidity ratio (SLR)
    89–90
stock posting 155
strategies, bank risk management
    11–12
stress scenarios, intraday liquidity
    risk 73–75, 82
stress testing
  contingency plans 34, 164, 166
  documentation-related liquidity
    risks 154
  governance principles 144, 147

internal capital and 122
long-term balance 111–122
  methodology 117–118
  rationale 113–117
  reverse stress testing 118–119
risk management 12
structural funding, long-term
  balance 94–99
structural needs, intraday
  liquidity risk 76–78
swaps 61
systemic risk, market liquidity 3

technology use, stress testing 115
temporary market impact,
  liquidation-adjusted VaR 134
term deposits 54
thin markets 131–132
tightness, market liquidity 132
time buckets 39–40, 87
time horizon, VaR
  liquidation-adjusted 133
time periods, stress testing 117
time series, stress testing 115–116
total net cash outflows 21–22
trade volume, asset liquidity
  measurement 89, 90
transaction costs,
  liquidation-adjusted VaR 135
transferability of funds, cash-flow
  ladder 44
transferability of liquidity 146
transparency, liquidity risk 32–33
treasury securities 110
triggers, covenants 27–28
trust 71, 73, 75

uncertainty 43, 64
unencumbered funds 19
unsecured market access 159
US Economic Policy Uncertainty
  indicator 64

valuation, complex financial
  derivatives 25
Value at Risk (VaR) 123–141
  exogenous/endogenous
    liquidity risk 137–138
  liquidation-adjusted 133–140
  market liquidity effects
    123–124
  market liquidity VaR 124–132
VIX (volatility index) 65
volatile fraction, non-maturity
  deposits 102
volatility 27, 124, 126
volatility index (VIX) 65

warning levels, liquidity risk
  162–163
Weighted Average Spread (WAS)
  138
weighted spread (*WS*), market
  liquidity 131
weighting factors 96–99
wholesale banks 22
wholesale funding 23–24
WS see weighted spread

yield curves, government bonds
  61

zero-coupon bonds 110